The watch you wear out there.

WITH FAST WRAP™ STRAPS

www.timex.com

cream OF THE crop

Front cover: Macaroni and Cheese, page 23; photography by Howard L. Puckett; styling by Melanie J. Clarke; food styling by Lorrie Hulston

Editor: **Alyson Moreland Haynes**
Art Director: **Fernande Bondarenko**
Managing Editor: **Kay Fuston**
Assistant Food Editor: **Regan Miller Jones, R.D.**
Copy Editor: **Maria Parker Hopkins**
Assistant Editor: **Kate McWhorter**
Contributing Editors: **Tami Pearce, Marge Perry**
Editorial Intern: **Emily Harrison**

Photographers: **Ralph Anderson, Jim Bathie, Tina Cornett, Colleen Duffley, Becky Luigart-Stayner, Randy Mayor, Howard L. Puckett**
Photo Stylists: **Cindy Manning Barr, Kay E. Clarke, Melanie J. Clarke, Virginia R. Cravens, Mary Catherine Muir, Fonda Shaia, Ashley J. Wyatt**

Weight Watchers Magazine Test Kitchens Director: **Kathleen Royal Phillips**
Assistant Director: **Gayle Hays Sadler** Staff: **Julie Christopher, Shelley Clayton, M.A., R.D., Lorrie Hulston, Natalie E. King, L. Victoria Knowles, Rebecca W. Mohr, Jan A. Smith, Kate M. Wheeler, R.D.**

Vice President, Editor, *Weight Watchers* Magazine: **Kate Greer**
Executive Editor: **Mary Kay Culpepper**
Art Director: **Amy Heise**
Assistant Art Director: **Craig Hyde**
Staff Stylist: **Rose Nguyen**
Editorial Coordinator: **Christine O'Connell**

Senior Vice President, Publisher: **Jeffrey C. Ward**
General Manager: **Vicki A. Denmark**
Business Manager: **Michael W. Stern**
Marketing Manager: **Betsey Hummel**
Production Manager: **Robin Boteler**

President and CEO: **Tom Angelillo**
Executive Vice Presidents: **Bruce Akin, Jeanetta Keller, Scott Sheppard**
Vice President, Administration: **Lane Schmitt**
Vice President, Corporate Marketing: **Greg Keyes**
Vice President, Consumer Marketing: **Pat Vander Meer**
Vice President, Finance: **Bruce Larson**
Vice President, Production: **Larry Rinehart**

Back cover: Fudgy Chocolate Brownies, page 92; photography by Howard L. Puckett; styling by Melanie J. Clarke; food styling by Julie Christopher

WELCOME

By the time a recipe appears in our magazine, it has been through the equivalent of a culinary Olympics. Each recipe is tested in our kitchens, tasted, rated on a variety of attributes (including flavor, texture, and appearance), and often reworked and tweaked many times until it's just right. The process can take weeks—all to make a single recipe the best it can be. Multiply that procedure by the volume of recipes we publish each year, and you can see that we keep our test kitchen associates and taste-testers pretty busy. We also end up with some spectacular recipes. These are the dishes we make at home, the ones we talk about and use as a standard for comparison. As many fabulous recipes as I see every day, I still salivate at the thought of Bittersweet Chocolate Pudding (page 82), and I make Quick-and-Easy Salisbury Steaks (page 9) regularly.

So we present this collection of our all-time-favorite, top-rated recipes. These are the dishes that received the highest scores from our tasting panel. In fact, throughout the book we've flagged the ones we consider the absolute "cream of the crop;" for a complete list of these favorites turn to page 94. You'll find a recipe perfect for every occasion, from our unbeatable main and side dishes to simply unforgettable desserts. Of course, our recipes follow strict nutritional criteria, so you know that enjoying these dishes will contribute to your overall good health.

To that end, each recipe includes ***POINTS***®, the basis for the Weight Watchers 1•2•3 Success® Weight Loss Plan. We also counted the calories, protein, fat, carbohydrates, fiber, cholesterol, iron, sodium, and calcium and included diabetic exchanges. As food editors and test kitchen associates, we see and taste an incredible variety of food. The recipes that follow are the ones we chose as the cream of the crop. We're sure you'll agree.

Alyson M. Haynes

cream
OF THE crop

c o n t e n t s

Editor's Choice Entrées

FINISH THE DAY ON A HIGH NOTE WITH ONE OF OUR SATISFYING MAIN DISHES.

For many of us who love to cook and eat, dinner is the highlight of the day. After hours of focusing on getting things done, dinnertime is often the first opportunity we have to pay attention to our needs and pleasures. What better way to celebrate the effort we put forth all day than by nourishing our bodies as we delight our senses. Whether you're having a quiet, casual meal for two, a lively family affair, or an elegant soiree with friends, you'll find just the right fare in the following recipes. From the unusual and beguiling Penne Puttanesca to the down-home Cowboy Pork Chops and Pinto Beans (both on page 22), there is truly a recipe for every occasion and every palate.

Garlic-Lover's Shrimp will satisfy the most ardent admirers of the garlic bulb.

Quick-and-Easy Salisbury Steaks

Garlic-Lover's Shrimp

Serve this with lots of crusty French bread.

1   tablespoon olive oil
¼   teaspoon crushed red pepper
8   garlic cloves, minced
1   bay leaf
1½ pounds large shrimp, peeled
¼   teaspoon salt
½   cup dry white wine
2   tablespoons minced fresh parsley
¼   teaspoon dried thyme

1. Heat oil in a large nonstick skillet over medium-high heat. Add pepper, garlic, and bay leaf; sauté 30 seconds. Add shrimp and salt; sauté 3 minutes. Remove shrimp from skillet; set aside. Add wine, parsley, and thyme to skillet; bring to a boil, and cook until reduced to ¼ cup (about 1 minute). Return shrimp to skillet; toss to coat. Discard bay leaf. Yield: 4 servings.

POINTS: 4; **Exchanges:** 3½ Very Lean Meat, 1 Fat
Per serving: CAL 177 (28% from fat); PRO 26.4g; FAT 5.6g (sat 0.9g); CARB 3.8g; FIB 0.2g; CHOL 194mg; IRON 3.5mg; SOD 340mg; CALC 84mg

Quick-and-Easy Salisbury Steaks

1   pound ground round
¼   teaspoon garlic powder
¼   teaspoon salt
¼   teaspoon pepper
Cooking spray
1   (8-ounce) package presliced fresh mushrooms
¼   cup chopped onion
1   tablespoon finely chopped fresh or 1 teaspoon dried thyme
2   tablespoons dry sherry or dry white wine
1   (12-ounce) jar fat-free beef gravy
Thyme sprigs (optional)

1. Combine first 4 ingredients; stir well. Shape mixture into 4 (½-inch-thick) patties.
2. Coat a large nonstick skillet with cooking spray; place over medium heat until hot. Add patties; cook 4 minutes on each side or until done. Remove patties from skillet, and set aside.
3. Increase heat to medium-high. Add mushrooms, onion, and thyme to skillet; sauté 3

minutes. Add sherry; sauté 1 minute. Stir in gravy; return patties to skillet. Cook 2 minutes or until thoroughly heated. Garnish with thyme sprigs, if desired. Yield: 4 servings.

POINTS: 5; **Exchanges:** 3 Lean Meat, 1 Veg, ½ Starch
Per serving: CAL 237 (24% from fat); PRO 29.2g; FAT 6.3g (sat 5.8g); CARB 13.7g; FIB 1.7g; CHOL 65mg; IRON 3.5mg; SOD 511mg; CALC 26mg

Barbecued-Chicken Potpie

1   teaspoon butter or stick margarine
Cooking spray
2   cups chopped onion
½   cup chopped green bell pepper
⅓   cup seeded diced poblano chile or 1 (4.5-ounce) can chopped green chiles, drained
1   small garlic clove, minced
1½ teaspoons cumin seeds
1   teaspoon ground coriander
¼   cup cider vinegar
4   cups cooked shredded chicken breast (about 1½ pounds)
2   tablespoons brown sugar
1   ounce unsweetened chocolate, grated
1   (12-ounce) bottle chili sauce
1   (10½-ounce) can low-salt chicken broth
1   (11.5-ounce) can refrigerated corn bread twists

1. Preheat oven to 375°.
2. Melt butter in a large nonstick skillet coated with cooking spray over medium-high heat. Add onion, bell pepper, chile, and garlic; sauté 5 minutes. Add cumin seeds and coriander; sauté 2 minutes. Stir in cider vinegar, scraping skillet to loosen browned bits. Add chicken and next 4 ingredients; cook 15 minutes or until thick, stirring occasionally. Spoon into an 11- x 7-inch baking dish coated with cooking spray.
3. Unroll corn bread dough, separating into strips. Place strips in a lattice fashion over chicken mixture. Bake at 375° for 25 minutes or until golden brown; let stand 15 minutes before serving. Yield: 8 servings.

POINTS: 9; **Exchanges:** 3½ Very Lean Meat, 2½ Starch, 1 Veg, 1 Fat
Per serving: CAL 394 (27% from fat); PRO 33.1g; FAT 12g (sat 3.7g); CARB 40g; FIB 1.7g; CHOL 78mg; IRON 3.5mg; SOD 972mg; CALC 49mg

Italian Turkey Burgers

4   (1½-ounce) sesame hamburger buns, split
Olive oil-flavored cooking spray
1   garlic clove, halved
1   pound ground turkey
½   cup tomato and basil pasta sauce (such as Barilla basilico)
⅓   cup finely chopped onion
¼   cup Italian-seasoned breadcrumbs
¼   cup (1 ounce) grated fresh Parmesan cheese
1   tablespoon chopped fresh parsley
2   (1-ounce) presliced part-skim mozzarella cheese slices, cut in half

1. Lightly coat cut sides of buns with cooking spray. Place buns, cut sides up, on a broiler pan. Broil 2 minutes or until lightly toasted. Rub garlic evenly over cut sides of buns. Discard garlic; set buns aside.

2. Combine turkey and next 5 ingredients in a bowl; stir well. Shape mixture into 4 (½-inch-thick) patties. Place on broiler pan; broil 7 minutes on each side or until done. Place patties on bottom halves of buns; top each with ½ cheese slice, and broil 1 minute or until cheese melts. Cover with tops of buns. Yield: 4 servings.

POINTS: 8; **Exchanges:** 4½ Very Lean Meat, 2 Starch, 1 Fat
Per serving: CAL 372 (22% from fat); FAT 9g (sat 4.1g); PRO 36.6g; CARB 33.8g; FIB 2g; CHOL 78mg; IRON 3.2mg; SOD 785mg; CALC 225mg

Fruited Cider Roast

1   (3½-pound) lean, boned top round roast
¼   teaspoon salt
¼   teaspoon pepper
Cooking spray
6   cups apple cider
3   cups cider vinegar
1   (6-ounce) package dried apricot halves, chopped
½   cup raisins
¼   cup firmly packed dark brown sugar
¼   teaspoon ground allspice

1. Trim fat from roast. Sprinkle salt and pepper evenly over roast. Coat a large Dutch oven with cooking spray; place over medium-high heat until hot. Add roast; cook until browned on all sides.

2. Pour cider and vinegar over roast. Bring to a boil; cover, reduce heat, and simmer 3 to 3½ hours or until roast is tender. Remove roast from pan, and place on a serving platter. Set aside, and keep warm.

3. Skim fat from pan juices. Reserve 2 cups juices; discard remaining juices. Return 2 cups juices to pan; add apricots and next 3 ingredients. Cook over medium-high heat 8 minutes or until thick, stirring frequently. Thinly slice roast; serve with fruit mixture. Yield: 12 servings (serving size: 3 ounces roast and one-twelfth fruit mixture).

POINTS: 5; **Exchanges:** 4 Very Lean Meat, 1½ Fruit, ½ Fat
Per serving: CAL 253 (20% from fat); PRO 28.4g; FAT 5.6g (sat 1.9g); CARB 22.5g; FIB 1.5g; CHOL 73mg; IRON 4.6mg; SOD 107mg; CALC 26mg

Speedy Chicken Parmesan

Served atop a plateful of pasta, this saucy dish is a hearty weeknight favorite.

4   (4-ounce) skinned, boned chicken breast halves
1   large egg, lightly beaten
½   cup Italian-seasoned breadcrumbs
1½ teaspoons butter or stick margarine, melted
Cooking spray
1¾ cups fire-roasted tomato and garlic pasta sauce (such as Classico)
½   cup (2 ounces) shredded part-skim mozzarella cheese
1   tablespoon grated Parmesan cheese
¼   cup chopped fresh parsley
3   cups hot cooked spaghetti (about 6 ounces uncooked pasta), cooked without salt or fat

1. Place chicken between 2 sheets of heavy-duty plastic wrap; flatten to ¼-inch thickness using a meat mallet or rolling pin. Dip chicken in egg, and dredge in breadcrumbs.

2. Melt butter in a large nonstick skillet coated with cooking spray over medium-high heat. Add chicken; cook 4 minutes on each side or until browned. Spoon pasta sauce over chicken; cover, reduce heat, and simmer 10 minutes. Sprinkle with cheeses and parsley; cover and simmer an additional 5 minutes or until cheeses melt. Spoon ¾ cup pasta onto each of 4 plates; top each with a chicken breast half. Divide sauce evenly over each serving. Yield: 4 servings.

POINTS: 10; **Exchanges:** 4 Very Lean Meat, 3 Starch, 1½ Veg, 1 Fat
Per serving: CAL 470 (20% from fat); PRO 41g; FAT 10.4g (sat 3.9g); CARB 49.7g; FIB 3.7g; CHOL 141mg; IRON 3.9mg; SOD 925mg; CALC 208mg

Caesar Chicken-Pasta Salad

3   cups (about 12 ounces) skinned, shredded roasted chicken breast (such as Tyson's)
3   cups cooked penne (about 6 ounces uncooked tubular-shaped pasta), cooked without salt or fat
2   cups thinly sliced romaine lettuce
1½ cups halved cherry tomatoes
½   cup thinly sliced fresh basil
½   cup chopped green onions
⅓   cup fat-free Caesar dressing
¼   cup chopped fresh parsley
1   (4-ounce) package crumbled feta cheese
1   garlic clove, minced

1. Combine all ingredients in a large bowl; toss well. Yield: 4 servings (serving size: 2 cups).

Note: To lower the sodium, use plain cooked chicken in place of the commercial roasted variety.

POINTS: 7; **Exchanges:** 2½ Starch, 1½ Med-fat Meat, 1 Veg, ½ Fat
Per serving: CAL 362 (22% from fat); PRO 19.4g; FAT 8.8g (sat 5.2g); CARB 40.4g; FIB 3.5g; CHOL 78mg; IRON 2.6mg; SOD 951mg; CALC 206mg

Marinated Flank Steak

1   (1½-pound) lean flank steak
¼   cup water
¼   cup dry red wine
¼   cup low-salt soy sauce
3   tablespoons lemon juice
1   tablespoon vegetable oil
1   teaspoon dried oregano
1   teaspoon cracked pepper
1   teaspoon dry mustard
2   teaspoons honey
¼   teaspoon salt
1   garlic clove, crushed

1. Trim fat from steak. Combine steak and remaining ingredients in a large zip-top plastic bag; seal bag. Refrigerate 8 hours, turning bag occasionally.
2. Prepare grill. Remove steak from bag, and discard marinade.

3. Place steak on grill rack; cover and grill 7 minutes on each side or until desired degree of doneness. Slice steak diagonally across grain into thin slices. Yield: 6 servings (serving size: 3 ounces).

POINTS: 6; **Exchanges:** 3 Lean Meat, 1 Fat
Per serving: CAL 230 (55% from fat); PRO 21.7g; FAT 14.1g (sat 5.5g); CARB 1.6g; FIB 0.1g; CHOL 60mg; IRON 2.3mg; SOD 250mg; CALC 9mg

Beef Stroganoff

1   pound lean, boned top sirloin steak
Cooking spray
1   (8-ounce) package presliced fresh mushrooms
1   small onion, cut in half lengthwise and sliced crosswise
2   garlic cloves, crushed
1   tablespoon all-purpose flour
½   cup water
¼   cup dry red wine

Caesar Chicken-Pasta Salad gets its savory flavor from roasted chicken.

until slightly thick, stirring occasionally. Remove from heat; stir in sour cream. Spoon 1 cup noodles onto each of 6 plates; top each serving evenly with steak mixture. Sprinkle with green onions. Yield: 6 servings.

POINTS: 8; **Exchanges:** 2 Lean Meat, 3 Starch, 1 Veg
Per serving: CAL 387 (23% from fat); PRO 26.4g; FAT 9.7g (sat 2.7g); CARB 46.7g; FIB 4.6g; CHOL 80mg; IRON 110mg; SOD 148mg; CALC 66mg

Grilled Orange Roughy With Pineapple-Cucumber Salsa

Pineapple-Cucumber Salsa
½   cup low-salt soy sauce
¼   cup fresh lime juice
3   tablespoons white rum (optional)
2   tablespoons honey
Dash of hot sauce
4   (4-ounce) orange roughy fillets
Cooking spray

1. Prepare Pineapple-Cucumber Salsa; set aside.
2. Combine soy sauce and next 4 ingredients in a shallow dish; stir well. Add fish, turning to coat. Cover and marinate in refrigerator 30 minutes.
3. Prepare grill. Remove fish from dish; discard marinade. Place fish on grill rack coated with cooking spray; cover and grill 4 minutes on each side or until fish flakes easily when tested with a fork. Serve with Pineapple-Cucumber Salsa. Yield: 4 servings (serving size: 1 fish fillet and ½ cup salsa).

POINTS: 5; **Exchanges:** 3 Lean Meat, 1 Fruit
Per serving: CAL 216 (29% from fat); PRO 22g; FAT 6.9g (sat 1g); CARB 14.5g; FIB 0.3g; CHOL 68mg; IRON 1.3mg; SOD 159mg; CALC 41mg

Pineapple-Cucumber Salsa:

1   (20-ounce) can pineapple tidbits in juice, drained
1½ cups chopped unwaxed salad cucumber
⅓   cup finely chopped red onion
2   tablespoons sugar
3   tablespoons fresh lime juice
⅛   teaspoon crushed red pepper

1. Combine all ingredients in a bowl; stir well. Serve at room temperature or chilled with grilled fish, chicken, or pork. Yield: 3½ cups.

A mild, sweet fish does a tangy rumba in Grilled Orange Roughy With Pineapple-Cucumber Salsa.

1   teaspoon dry mustard
1   teaspoon beef-flavored bouillon granules
½   teaspoon dried thyme
¼   teaspoon pepper
½   cup low-fat sour cream
6   cups hot cooked medium egg noodles, cooked without salt or fat
2   tablespoons sliced green onions

1. Trim fat from steak; cut steak diagonally across grain into ¼-inch-thick slices.
2. Coat a large nonstick skillet with cooking spray; place over medium-high heat until hot. Add steak, mushrooms, onion, and garlic; sauté until steak is browned. Drain; return to skillet.
3. Place flour in a small bowl. Gradually add water, stirring with a whisk until blended. Stir in wine and next 4 ingredients. Add flour mixture to steak mixture; bring to a boil. Cover, reduce heat, and simmer 10 minutes, stirring occasionally. Uncover and cook an additional 5 minutes or

Sesame Broccoli Stir-Fry

Cooking spray
1   tablespoon dark sesame oil
1   (12.3-ounce) package firm low-fat tofu,
    drained and cubed
4   cups fresh broccoli florets
1½ cups diced red bell pepper
¼   cup low-salt soy sauce
3   cups hot cooked instant brown rice,
    cooked without salt and fat
1½ tablespoons sesame seeds, toasted

1. Coat a wok or large nonstick skillet with cooking spray; add oil, and place over medium-high heat until hot. Add tofu; stir-fry 5 minutes or until lightly browned. Remove tofu from wok; set aside, and keep warm.

2. Add broccoli, bell pepper, and soy sauce to wok; stir-fry 3 minutes or until vegetables are crisp-tender. Add tofu, and stir-fry 30 seconds or until thoroughly heated.

3. Spoon ¾ cup rice onto each of 4 plates; top evenly with broccoli mixture. Sprinkle evenly with sesame seeds. Yield: 4 servings.

POINTS: 6; **Exchanges:** 2½ Very Lean Meat, 1½ Starch, 2 Veg, 1 Fat
Per serving: CAL 302 (29% from fat); PRO 21.4g; FAT 9.6g (sat 0.7g); CARB 42.1g; FIB 6.6g; CHOL 0mg; IRON 2.5mg; SOD 484mg; CALC 79mg

Lemon-Garlic Chicken Thighs

This chicken dish bakes in its marinade for added flavor. And it's made in one dish for easy cleanup.

¼   cup fresh lemon juice
2   tablespoons molasses
2   teaspoons Worcestershire sauce
4   garlic cloves, chopped
Cooking spray
8   chicken thighs (about 2 pounds), skinned
¼   teaspoon salt
¼   teaspoon pepper

1. Combine first 4 ingredients in an 11- x 7-inch baking dish coated with cooking spray; stir well. Add chicken, turning to coat. Cover; marinate in refrigerator 1 hour, turning chicken occasionally.
2. Preheat oven to 425°.
3. Sprinkle salt and pepper evenly over chicken. Bake at 425° for 40 minutes or until chicken is done, basting chicken occasionally. Yield: 4 servings (serving size: 2 chicken thighs).

POINTS: 6; **Exchanges:** 3½ Lean Meat, ½ Starch, ½ Fat
Per serving: CAL 258 (40% from fat); PRO 27.3g; FAT 11.6g (sat 3.3g); CARB 9.9g; FIB 0.1g; CHOL 98mg; IRON 1.9mg; SOD 268mg; CALC 43mg

Three-Pepper Pork Cutlets

1   (1-pound) pork tenderloin
2   teaspoons sweet Hungarian paprika
1   teaspoon dried thyme
1   teaspoon olive oil
½   teaspoon dried oregano
½   teaspoon dried rosemary, crushed
¼   teaspoon salt
¼   teaspoon ground white pepper
¼   teaspoon freshly ground black pepper
⅛   teaspoon ground red pepper
2   garlic cloves, minced
Cooking spray

1. Trim fat from pork. Cut pork crosswise into 8 slices. Place pork slices between 2 sheets of heavy-duty plastic wrap, and flatten each slice to ¼-inch thickness using a meat mallet or rolling pin.

2. Combine paprika and next 9 ingredients in a small bowl; stir well. Rub spice mixture evenly over both sides of pork slices.

3. Place pork slices on a broiler pan coated with cooking spray, and broil 4 minutes on each side or until done. Yield: 4 servings (serving size: 3 ounces).

POINTS: 4; **Exchanges:** 4 Very Lean Meat
Per serving: CAL 172 (31% from fat); PRO 26.9g; FAT 5.9g (sat 1.7g); CARB 1.8g; FIB 0.4g; CHOL 86mg; IRON 2.3mg; SOD 209mg; CALC 26mg

Mediterranean Pasta

4   cups chopped tomato
2   tablespoons chopped fresh basil
1   tablespoon olive oil
1   tablespoon red wine vinegar
¼   teaspoon salt
⅛   teaspoon crushed red pepper
1   garlic clove, minced
4   cups cooked angel hair (about 8 ounces
    uncooked pasta), cooked without
    salt or fat
¼   cup (1 ounce) crumbled feta cheese

1. Combine first 7 ingredients in a large bowl, and stir well. Let stand 10 minutes. Serve at room temperature over cooked pasta, and sprinkle with crumbled feta. Yield: 4 servings (serving size: 1 cup tomato mixture, 1 cup pasta, and 1 tablespoon cheese).

POINTS: 5; **Exchanges:** 3 Veg, 2 Starch, 1 Fat
Per serving: CAL 286 (20% from fat); PRO 9.3g; FAT 6.4g (sat 1.7g); CARB 48.8g; FIB 4.6g; CHOL 6mg; IRON 2.9mg; SOD 243mg; CALC 58mg

Make-Ahead Breakfast Casserole

¾ pound lean ground pork
¾ teaspoon dried Italian seasoning
¼ teaspoon fennel seeds, crushed
2 garlic cloves, minced
1 cup skim milk
¼ cup (1 ounce) shredded cheddar cheese
¾ teaspoon dry mustard
½ teaspoon salt
½ teaspoon ground red pepper
3 green onions, chopped
2 (8-ounce) cartons egg substitute
6 (1-ounce) slices white bread, cut into ½-inch cubes
Cooking spray
Thyme sprigs (optional)

1. Cook ground pork, Italian seasoning, fennel seeds, and minced garlic in a large nonstick skillet over medium heat until pork is browned, stirring to crumble. Drain; set aside.
2. Combine milk and next 6 ingredients in a large bowl; stir with a whisk until well blended. Add pork mixture and bread cubes, stirring until well blended. Pour into an 11- x 7-inch baking dish coated with cooking spray. Cover and chill 8 to 12 hours.
3. Preheat oven to 350°.
4. Bake, uncovered, at 350° for 50 minutes or until set and lightly browned. Garnish with thyme, if desired. Yield: 6 servings.

POINTS: 6; **Exchanges:** 3 Lean Meat, 1 Starch
Per serving: CAL 258 (31% from fat); PRO 24.2g; FAT 8.8g (sat 3.3g); CARB 18.8g; FIB 0.8g; CHOL 45mg; IRON 2.9mg; SOD 436mg; CALC 148mg

EDITOR'S CHOICE

Lime-Basted Pork Chops With Plum Relish

½ cup fresh lime juice, divided
⅓ cup finely chopped plum
2 tablespoons finely chopped tomato
1 tablespoon brown sugar
1 tablespoon finely chopped green onions
2 drops hot sauce
2 (4-ounce) boned center-cut pork loin chops (about ¾ inch thick)
1 teaspoon chopped fresh thyme
⅛ teaspoon salt
⅛ teaspoon pepper
Cooking spray

1. Combine ½ teaspoon lime juice, plums, and next 4 ingredients; stir well. Cover relish, and chill.
2. Place chops between 2 sheets of heavy-duty plastic wrap; flatten to ½-inch thickness using a meat mallet or rolling pin. Place chops in a shallow dish; add remaining lime juice, thyme, salt, and pepper. Cover and marinate in refrigerator 1 hour, turning chops occasionally.
3. Prepare grill. Remove chops from dish, reserving marinade. Place chops on grill rack coated with cooking spray; cover and grill 6 minutes on each side or until done, basting occasionally with reserved marinade. Serve chops with plum relish. Yield: 2 servings (serving size: 1 pork chop and ¼ cup relish).

POINTS: 6; **Exchanges:** 3½ Lean Meat, 1 Fruit, ½ Fat
Per serving: CAL 274 (39% from fat); PRO 25.1g; FAT 11.8g (sat 3.9g); CARB 17.8g; FIB 1.2g; CHOL 77mg; IRON 2.2mg; SOD 207mg; CALC 38mg

Turkey Cutlets in Wine

½ cup all-purpose flour
¼ cup grated Parmesan cheese
½ teaspoon paprika
¼ teaspoon salt
¼ teaspoon pepper
1 pound turkey breast cutlets (about 6 cutlets)
1 tablespoon olive oil, divided
1 tablespoon butter or stick margarine, divided
½ cup dry Marsala wine
2 tablespoons lemon juice
1 teaspoon garlic powder

Make-Ahead Breakfast Casserole

Spinach-and-Roasted Red Pepper Pizza

Cooking spray
1 tablespoon cornmeal
1 (10-ounce) can refrigerated pizza crust dough
1 cup (4 ounces) shredded Asiago cheese, divided
¼ teaspoon ground nutmeg
⅛ teaspoon pepper
1 (10-ounce) package frozen chopped spinach, thawed, drained, and squeezed dry
1 (7-ounce) bottle roasted red bell peppers, drained and cut into 2-inch strips
½ teaspoon dried thyme

1. Preheat oven to 425°.

2. Coat a 12-inch round pizza pan with cooking spray, and sprinkle with cornmeal. Pat pizza crust dough into prepared pan.

3. Combine ½ cup cheese, nutmeg, pepper, and spinach in a bowl; toss well. Spread spinach mixture over dough. Top with bell pepper strips; sprinkle with thyme and remaining ½ cup cheese. Bake at 425° for 15 minutes or until crust is browned and cheese melts. Yield: 6 servings.

POINTS: 5; **Exchanges:** 1½ Starch, 1 Veg, ½ Fat, ½ Lean Meat
Per serving: CAL 218 (28% from fat); PRO 8.9g; FAT 6.8g (sat 3.5g); CARB 26.4g; FIB 1.6g; CHOL 20mg; IRON 1.2mg; SOD 565mg; CALC 256mg

Tuna Noodle Casserole

Cooking spray
¾ cup sliced fresh mushrooms
¼ cup chopped red bell pepper
2 tablespoons finely chopped onion
3 tablespoons stick margarine
3 tablespoons all-purpose flour
2 cups skim milk
4 cups cooked medium egg noodles (about 4 cups uncooked), cooked without salt or fat
1 cup frozen green peas, thawed
¼ teaspoon salt
⅛ teaspoon pepper
1 (9-ounce) can solid white tuna in water, drained and flaked
¼ cup dry breadcrumbs
½ cup (2 ounces) shredded sharp cheddar cheese

Pump a little iron and pack a lot of flavor with Spinach-and-Roasted Red Pepper Pizza.

1. Combine first 5 ingredients in a shallow dish; stir well. Dredge turkey cutlets in flour mixture.

2. Place 1½ teaspoons oil and 1½ teaspoons butter in a large nonstick skillet over medium-high heat until butter melts. Add 3 turkey cutlets, and cook 4 minutes on each side or until browned. Remove turkey from skillet, and set aside. Repeat procedure with remaining oil, butter, and turkey, and set aside.

3. Add Marsala, lemon juice, and garlic powder to drippings in skillet. Cook over medium-high heat until mixture is bubbly, stirring constantly; reduce heat to medium, and return turkey to skillet. Cook 2 minutes or until thoroughly heated. Yield: 4 servings.

POINTS: 6; **Exchanges:** 3½ Very Lean Meat, 1 Starch, 1 Fat
Per serving: CAL 255 (31% from fat); PRO 29.4g; FAT 8.6g (sat 3.4g); CARB 13.5g; FIB 0.5g; CHOL 82mg; IRON 2.3mg; SOD 316mg; CALC 90mg

1. Preheat oven to 350°.

2. Coat a medium saucepan with cooking spray; place over medium heat until hot. Add mushrooms, bell pepper, and onion; sauté 3 minutes. Drain in a colander; set aside.

3. Melt margarine in pan over medium-low heat. Add flour, stirring with a whisk until blended. Cook 1 minute, stirring constantly. Reduce heat to medium. Gradually add milk, stirring constantly. Cook 6 minutes or until mixture is thick and bubbly, stirring occasionally. Pour into a large bowl; stir in mushroom mixture, noodles, and next 4 ingredients.

4. Spoon into a shallow 2-quart baking dish coated with cooking spray; top with breadcrumbs and cheese. Cover and bake at 350° for 30 minutes; uncover and bake an additional 5 minutes or until cheese melts. Yield: 8 servings (serving size: 1 cup).

POINTS: 6; **Exchanges:** 2 Starch, 2 Very Lean Meat, 1 Fat
Per serving: CAL 289 (28% from fat); PRO 19.9g; FAT 9g (sat 2.8g); CARB 32g; FIB 2.9g; CHOL 51mg; IRON 2.3mg; SOD 424mg; CALC 188mg

Ham-and-Grits Casserole

4   cups water
¼   teaspoon salt
1   cup uncooked quick-cooking grits
1   cup chopped lean, lower-salt ham
3   tablespoons reduced-calorie stick margarine
1   teaspoon low-salt Worcestershire sauce
1   (8-ounce) carton egg substitute
Cooking spray
½   cup (2 ounces) shredded reduced-fat sharp cheddar cheese

1. Preheat oven to 350°.

2. Bring 4 cups water and salt to a boil in a large saucepan; stir in grits. Cover, reduce heat, and simmer 5 minutes or until thick, stirring occasionally. Remove from heat. Add ham, margarine, and Worcestershire sauce; stir until margarine melts. Gradually add egg substitute, stirring constantly.

3. Spoon into an 11- x 7- inch baking dish coated

with cooking spray. Bake, uncovered, at 350° for 45 minutes. Sprinkle with cheese. Bake an additional 5 minutes or until cheese melts. Let stand 5 minutes before serving. Yield: 8 servings (serving size: ¾ cup).

POINTS: 4; **Exchanges:** 1½ Starch, 1 Lean Meat
Per serving: CAL 166 (29% from fat); PRO 10.6g; FAT 5.3g (sat 1.8g); CARB 19.5g; FIB 1.1g; CHOL 14mg; IRON 1.3mg; SOD 365mg; CALC 68mg

Scallops Over Creamed Spinach

Cooking spray
1   cup sliced fresh mushrooms
⅓   cup tub-style light cream cheese, softened
3   tablespoons skim milk
2   tablespoons reduced-fat pesto-Parmesan salad dressing (such as Maple Grove Farms)
¼   teaspoon pepper
1   (10-ounce) package frozen chopped spinach, thawed, drained, and squeezed dry
1   pound sea scallops
1½   tablespoons grated Parmesan cheese

1. Preheat oven to 375°.

2. Coat a large nonstick skillet with cooking spray; place over medium-high heat until hot. Add mushrooms; sauté until tender. Drain in a colander; set aside.

3. Combine cream cheese and next 3 ingredients in a bowl; beat at medium speed of a mixer until smooth. Stir in mushrooms and spinach. Spoon mixture into 4 individual gratin dishes coated with cooking spray; set aside.

4. Recoat skillet with cooking spray; place over medium-high heat until hot. Add scallops; sauté 3 minutes. Spoon scallops evenly over spinach mixture in gratin dishes; sprinkle evenly with Parmesan cheese. Bake at 375° for 15 minutes or until thoroughly heated and lightly browned. Yield: 4 servings.

POINTS: 4; **Exchanges:** 3 Very Lean Meat, ½ Starch, ½ Veg, ½ Fat
Per serving: CAL 203 (31% from fat); PRO 25.0g; FAT 7g (sat 2.9g); CARB 9.9g; FIB 2.6g; CHOL 51mg; IRON 2.1mg; SOD 475mg; CALC 178mg

Egg-and-Tuna Salad Sandwiches

4   hard-cooked large eggs, chopped
1   (6-ounce) can chunk light tuna in water, drained and flaked
2   tablespoons minced red onion
3   tablespoons light mayonnaise
2   tablespoons Dijon mustard
½   teaspoon freshly ground pepper
10 (1-ounce) slices whole-wheat bread
5   large red leaf lettuce leaves
5   (¼-inch-thick) slices tomato
1¼ cups alfalfa sprouts

1. Combine first 6 ingredients in a medium bowl; stir well. Spread ½ cup egg mixture over each of 5 bread slices. Top each with 1 lettuce leaf, 1 tomato slice, ¼ cup alfalfa sprouts, and 1 bread slice. Yield: 5 servings.

POINTS: 6; **Exchanges:** 2 Starch, 1½ Very Lean Meat, 1 Veg
Per serving: CAL 294 (30% from fat); PRO 19.5g; FAT 9.8g (sat 2.3g); CARB 34.8g; FIB 4.8g; CHOL 184mg; IRON 4mg; SOD 697mg; CALC 176mg

Deviled Chicken Breasts

4   (4-ounce) skinned, boned chicken breast halves
¼   cup Italian-seasoned breadcrumbs
1   tablespoon olive oil
½   cup dry white wine
½   teaspoon dried savory, crushed, or dried thyme
¼   teaspoon salt
¼   teaspoon coarsely ground pepper
1   (4-ounce) jar whole mushrooms, drained
1   tablespoon honey mustard
1   tablespoon lemon juice

1. Dredge chicken in breadcrumbs. Heat oil in a large nonstick skillet over medium heat. Add chicken, and cook 3 minutes on each side or until browned. Add wine and next 4 ingredients; cover, reduce heat, and simmer 15 minutes or until chicken is done. Remove chicken and mushrooms from skillet with a slotted spoon, and place on a serving platter. Stir mustard and lemon juice into wine mixture in skillet, and cook 1 minute. Spoon sauce over chicken. Yield: 4 servings (serving size: 1 chicken breast half and 1 tablespoon sauce).

POINTS: 5; **Exchanges:** 3½ Very Lean Meat, ½ Starch, ½ Veg, ½ Fat
Per serving: CAL 215 (21% from fat); PRO 27.8g; FAT 5g (sat 0.9g); CARB 8.4g; FIB 0.3g; CHOL 66mg; IRON 1.5mg; SOD 548mg; CALC 29mg

Lamb-and-Eggplant Pizzas

Pizza for two is a cinch with ready-made "crusts" and imaginative toppings. This recipe pairs pitas with lamb, eggplant, and feta for a taste of the Middle East.

6   ounces lean ground lamb
2½ cups peeled cubed eggplant (about ½ pound)
⅓   cup water
½   teaspoon dried oregano
½   teaspoon lemon juice
¼   teaspoon garlic powder
⅓   cup Italian-style tomato paste
2   (8-inch) pita bread rounds, toasted
3   tablespoons (¾ ounce) crumbled feta cheese

1. Cook lamb in a large nonstick skillet over medium-high heat until browned, stirring to crumble. Drain in a colander; set aside.

2. Place skillet over medium-high heat until hot. Add eggplant cubes, and sauté 2 minutes. Add ⅓ cup water, oregano, lemon juice, and garlic powder; stir well. Cover, reduce heat, and simmer 5 minutes. Increase heat to high; uncover and cook 1 minute. Remove from heat; stir in lamb and tomato paste.

3. Place pita rounds on a baking sheet. Spread lamb mixture evenly over pita rounds, and top with cheese. Broil 2 minutes or until cheese softens. Yield: 2 servings.

POINTS: 5; **Exchanges:** 2½ Starch, 2 Veg, 2 Med-fat Meat
Per serving: CAL 386 (25% from fat); PRO 25.5g; FAT 10.7g (sat 4.2g); CARB 45.6g; FIB 9.1g; CHOL 68mg; IRON 5.1mg; SOD 456mg; CALC 195mg

Spicy Bistro Steak Subs

1   tablespoon stick margarine
2   garlic cloves, minced
1   pound thinly sliced lean deli roast beef
2   tablespoons ketchup
4   teaspoons Worcestershire sauce
½   teaspoon dried basil

EDITOR'S CHOICE

½ teaspoon dried oregano
¼ teaspoon ground red pepper
1 (12-ounce) can dark beer
6 (2½-ounce) hoagie rolls with sesame seeds, cut in half lengthwise
Carrot curls and olives (optional)

1. Melt margarine in a large nonstick skillet over medium-high heat. Add garlic; sauté 2 minutes. Add roast beef and next 6 ingredients; bring to a boil. Reduce heat, and simmer 2 minutes, stirring frequently. Drain roast beef in a colander over a bowl, reserving sauce. Divide roast beef evenly among roll bottoms, and top with roll tops. Serve sandwiches with reserved sauce. Garnish sandwiches with carrot curls and olives, if desired. Yield: 6 servings (serving size: 1 sandwich and 3 tablespoons sauce).

POINTS: 7; **Exchanges:** 2½ Starch, 2 Med-fat Meat
Per serving: CAL 345 (28% from fat); PRO 21.4g; FAT 10.6g (sat 3.4g); CARB 40.6g; FIB 1.6g; CHOL 2mg; IRON 3.8mg; SOD 938mg; CALC 67mg

Baked Buffalo Chicken

Cooking spray
4 (4-ounce) skinned, boned chicken breast halves
¼ cup hot sauce
1 tablespoon white vinegar
1 tablespoon stick margarine, melted
1 teaspoon celery seeds
⅛ teaspoon pepper
½ cup fat-free blue cheese dressing

1. Preheat oven to 400°.
2. Coat a large nonstick skillet with cooking spray; place over medium-high heat until hot. Add chicken; cook 4 minutes on each side or until browned. Place chicken in an 11- x 7-inch baking dish coated with cooking spray.
3. Combine hot sauce and next 4 ingredients; pour over chicken. Bake, uncovered, at 400° for 25 minutes. Serve with blue cheese dressing. Yield: 4 servings (serving size: 1 breast half and 2 tablespoons dressing).

POINTS: 5; **Exchanges:** 3 Very Lean Meat, 1 Starch, ½ Fat
Per serving: CAL 231 (26% from fat); PRO 27.7g; FAT 6.7g (sat 1.4g); CARB 13.6g; FIB 0.7g; CHOL 72mg; IRON 1.2mg; SOD 443mg; CALC 24mg

Ziti Casserole

½ pound ground chuck
½ pound ground turkey breast
Cooking spray
1 cup chopped onion
1 cup sliced fresh mushrooms
¾ cup chopped green bell pepper
2 garlic cloves, minced
1 cup water
¼ cup chopped fresh parsley
1½ teaspoons dried Italian seasoning
½ teaspoon pepper
¼ teaspoon salt
2 (14½-ounce) cans diced tomatoes, undrained
1 (6-ounce) can Italian-style tomato paste
3 cups cooked ziti (about 2¼ cups uncooked short tubular pasta), cooked without salt or fat
½ cup (2 ounces) grated fresh Parmesan cheese

1. Preheat oven to 375°.
2. Cook ground chuck and turkey in a Dutch oven over medium-high heat until browned,

Spicy Bistro Steak Subs take a dip in peppery beer sauce.

stirring until meat crumbles. Drain in a colander, and set aside.

3. Coat pan with cooking spray, and place over medium-high heat until hot. Add onion, mushrooms, bell pepper, and garlic; sauté until vegetables are tender. Return meat mixture to pan. Add water and next 6 ingredients; bring to a boil. Reduce heat, and simmer, uncovered, 25 minutes, stirring occasionally. Remove from heat, and stir in pasta.

4. Spoon into a 13- x 9-inch baking dish coated with cooking spray. Cover and bake at 375° for 25 minutes or until thoroughly heated. Sprinkle with Parmesan cheese. Cover loosely, and let stand 5 minutes or until cheese melts. Yield: 8 servings (serving size: 1⅓ cups).

POINTS: 5; **Exchanges:** 2 Veg, 1 Starch, 1 Med-fat Meat, 1 Fat **Per serving:** CAL 251 (32% from fat); PRO 16.8g; FAT 8.8g (sat 3.3g); CARB 26.5g; FIB 3.3g; CHOL 34mg; IRON 3.4mg; SOD 342mg; CALC 122mg

Goat Cheese Quesadillas With Green-Chile Salsa

It's hard to beat fresh salsa, but you may substitute a good-quality prepared salsa to reduce the prep time of this entrée. We recommend Herdez salsa casera.

1 (4-ounce) package goat cheese (about 1 cup), softened
1 cup (4 ounces) shredded reduced-fat Monterey Jack cheese
¼ cup chopped fresh cilantro
1 tablespoon chili powder
1 (15-ounce) can red beans, rinsed and drained
8 (8-inch) fat-free flour tortillas
Cooking spray
Green-Chile Salsa
Cilantro sprigs (optional)

1. Preheat oven to 350°.
2. Combine first 5 ingredients in a bowl; stir well. Spread about ¾ cup cheese mixture over each of 4 tortillas, leaving a ½-inch border. Top each with a tortilla, pressing gently. Place quesadillas on a large baking sheet coated with cooking spray; cover with foil. Bake at 350° for 25 min-

utes or until cheese melts. Cut each quesadilla into 4 wedges, if desired. Serve with Green-Chile Salsa; garnish with cilantro sprigs, if desired. Yield: 4 servings (serving size: 1 quesadilla and ⅓ cup salsa).

POINTS: 10; **Exchanges:** 4½ Starch, 1½ Very Lean Meat, 1½ Fat **Per serving:** CAL 477 (23% from fat); PRO 23g; FAT 12.4g (sat 7.5g); CARB 70.7g; FIB 4.3g; CHOL 44mg; IRON 2.9mg; SOD 1323mg; CALC 402mg

Green-Chile Salsa:

1⅓ cups seeded diced tomato
¼ cup diced sweet onion
1 teaspoon minced fresh cilantro
2 teaspoons fresh lime juice
¼ teaspoon freshly ground pepper
1 (4.5-ounce) can chopped green chiles

1. Combine all ingredients in a bowl. Serve at room temperature. Yield: 1⅓ cups.

Basil Grilled Lamb Chops

Marinate these chops longer than 2 hours for a more intense flavor.

8 (5-ounce) lean lamb loin chops (about 1 inch thick)
½ cup minced fresh onion
¼ cup honey
3 tablespoons chopped fresh basil
1½ tablespoons soy sauce
1 tablespoon vegetable oil
1 tablespoon minced fresh garlic
1 teaspoon salt
1 teaspoon freshly ground pepper

1. Trim fat from lamb chops. Set chops aside.
2. Combine minced onion and next 7 ingredients in a large zip-top plastic bag. Add chops; seal bag, and marinate in refrigerator at least 2 hours, turning bag occasionally.
3. Prepare grill. Remove lamb chops from plastic bag, reserving marinade. Place chops on grill rack, and grill 5 minutes on each side or until desired degree of doneness, basting frequently with reserved marinade. Yield: 8 servings.

POINTS: 6; **Exchanges:** 3½ Lean Meat, ½ Starch, ½ Fat **Per serving:** CAL 239 (38% from fat); PRO 25.9g; FAT 10g (sat 3.3g); CARB 10.5g; FIB 0.3g; CHOL 81mg; IRON 1.9mg; SOD 521mg; CALC 24mg

Goat Cheese Quesadillas With
Green-Chile Salsa

dish coated with cooking spray. Spoon tomato mixture over squash mixture. Combine remaining ¼ cup cheese and breadcrumbs, and sprinkle over tomato mixture. Bake at 450° for 15 minutes or until bubbly. Yield: 6 servings (serving size: about 1 cup).

POINTS: 3; **Exchanges:** 2½ Veg, 1 Fat, ½ Starch
Per serving: CAL 142 (28% from fat); PRO 7.7g; FAT 4.4g (sat 0.3g); CARB 20.2g; FIB 2.4g; CHOL 8mg; IRON 2.3mg; SOD 467mg; CALC 183mg

Cowboy Pork Chops and Pinto Beans

Serve with zucchini, watermelon wedges, and barbecue bread.

2   teaspoons ground cumin, divided
½   cup salsa
¼   cup barbecue sauce
2   green onions, sliced
1   (16-ounce) can pinto beans, undrained
4   (6-ounce) center-cut loin pork chops
½   teaspoon garlic powder
¼   teaspoon salt
¼   teaspoon ground red pepper
Cooking spray

1. Combine 1 teaspoon cumin, salsa, and next 3 ingredients in a medium saucepan. Bring to a boil. Reduce heat, and simmer 8 minutes, stirring occasionally. Remove from heat; set aside, and keep warm.

2. Trim fat from chops. Combine remaining 1 teaspoon cumin, garlic powder, salt, and pepper; sprinkle over both sides of chops. Place chops on a broiler pan coated with cooking spray; broil 5 minutes on each side or until done. Serve with beans. Yield: 4 servings (serving size: 1 chop and ¾ cup beans).

POINTS: 7; **Exchanges:** 3 Med-Fat Meat, 1 Starch, 1 Veg
Per serving: CAL 317 (34% from fat); PRO 28.6g; FAT 12.1g (sat 3.7g); CARB 22.6g; FIB 1g; CHOL 72mg; IRON 3.9mg; SOD 415mg; CALC 76mg

Penne Puttanesca

2   (14.5-ounce) cans no-salt-added diced tomatoes, undrained
Cooking spray
1   cup chopped green onions

Cowboy Pork Chops and Pinto Beans will be the belle of the barbecue, but it's hearty enough for a cowhand.

Spaghetti Squash-and-Vegetable Gratin

1   teaspoon olive oil
3   cups diced zucchini
3   cups sliced fresh mushrooms
¾   cup (3 ounces) shredded part-skim mozzarella cheese, divided
¼   cup chopped fresh parsley
¼   teaspoon salt
¼   teaspoon pepper
2   garlic cloves, minced
1   (14.5-ounce) can stewed tomatoes, undrained and chopped
3   cups cooked spaghetti squash
Cooking spray
½   cup fresh breadcrumbs

1. Preheat oven to 450°.

2. Heat olive oil in a large nonstick skillet over medium-high heat. Add zucchini and mushrooms; sauté 10 minutes. Remove from heat; stir in ¼ cup mozzarella cheese, chopped parsley, and next 4 ingredients.

3. Combine squash and ¼ cup cheese, and stir well. Spoon into a shallow 1½-quart baking

4 canned anchovy fillets, drained and finely chopped, or 2 teaspoons anchovy paste
½ cup dry white wine
¼ cup chopped pitted niçoise olives
2 tablespoons capers
2 teaspoons dried marjoram
¼ teaspoon pepper
4 garlic cloves, minced
5 cups hot cooked penne (about 12 ounces uncooked tubular-shaped pasta), cooked without salt or fat
5 tablespoons grated Parmesan cheese

1. Drain tomatoes, reserving ½ cup juice. Set both aside.

2. Coat a large nonstick skillet with cooking spray, and place over medium-low heat. Add green onions and anchovies; sauté 3 minutes. Increase heat to medium. Add tomatoes, reserved tomato juice, wine, and next 5 ingredients; cook 8 minutes or until reduced to 2½ cups. Spoon sauce over pasta, and sprinkle with cheese. Yield: 5 servings (serving size: 1 cup pasta, ½ cup sauce, and 1 tablespoon cheese).

POINTS: 4; **Exchanges:** 2 Starch, 2 Veg, ½ Fat
Per serving: CAL 229 (15% from fat); FAT 3.9g (sat 1.5g); PRO 10g; CARB 39.2g; FIB 2.5g; CHOL 5mg; IRON 2.9mg; SOD 742mg; CALC 168mg

Spaghetti-Ham Pie

Cooking spray
¾ cup chopped lean, lower-salt ham
¾ cup sliced fresh mushrooms
½ teaspoon minced garlic
2 tablespoons all-purpose flour
¼ teaspoon salt
⅛ teaspoon pepper
1 (12-ounce) can evaporated skim milk
3 cups cooked spaghetti (about 6 ounces uncooked pasta), cooked without salt or fat
1 cup (4 ounces) finely shredded reduced-fat Swiss cheese, divided

1. Preheat oven to 425°.

2. Coat a large nonstick skillet with cooking spray, and place over medium-high heat until hot. Add ham, mushrooms, and garlic; sauté until mushrooms are tender. Stir in flour, salt, and pepper; cook 1 minute, stirring constantly.

Gradually add milk, stirring constantly. Cook over medium heat until mixture is thick, stirring occasionally. Remove from heat; stir in pasta and ½ cup Swiss cheese.

3. Spoon into a 9-inch pie plate coated with cooking spray, and sprinkle with remaining ½ cup Swiss cheese. Bake, uncovered, at 425° for 15 minutes. Let stand 5 minutes. Cut into 6 wedges. Yield: 6 servings.

POINTS: 5; **Exchanges:** 2 Starch, 2 Very Lean Meat
Per serving: CAL 245 (19% from fat); PRO 18.3g; FAT 5.1g (sat 2.3g); CARB 31.1g; FIB 0.9g; CHOL 23mg; IRON 1.7mg; SOD 341mg; CALC 354mg

Macaroni and Cheese

4 cups hot cooked elbow macaroni (about 8 ounces uncooked), cooked without salt or fat
2 cups (8 ounces) shredded reduced-fat sharp cheddar cheese
1 cup 1% low-fat cottage cheese
¾ cup fat-free sour cream
½ cup skim milk
2 tablespoons grated fresh onion
1½ teaspoons reduced-calorie stick margarine, melted
½ teaspoon salt
¼ teaspoon pepper
1 large egg, lightly beaten
Cooking spray
¼ cup fresh or dry breadcrumbs
1 tablespoon reduced-calorie stick margarine, melted
¼ teaspoon paprika

1. Preheat oven to 350°.

2. Combine first 10 ingredients; stir well. Spoon into a shallow 2-quart casserole coated with cooking spray.

3. Combine breadcrumbs, 1 tablespoon margarine, and paprika; stir well. Sprinkle breadcrumb mixture over casserole. Cover and bake at 350° for 45 minutes. Uncover casserole; bake an additional 5 minutes or until breadcrumbs are lightly browned. Yield: 6 servings (serving size: 1 cup).

POINTS: 8; **Exchanges:** 2 Starch, 1½ Lean Meat, 1 L-F Milk
Per serving: CAL 356 (28% from fat); PRO 24.9g; FAT 11.2g (sat 5.2g); CARB 37.5g; FIB 1.2g; CHOL 63mg; IRON 2mg; SOD 724mg; CALC 402mg

Five-Star Soups and Stews

Garden Gazpacho keeps the kitchen cool: This uncooked soup, made from puréed vegetables, is served cold.

*S*oups and stews are universally beloved. Every country or region seems to have one it holds dear. In this chapter, you'll find recipes from all over the globe: France's Soupe à l'Oignon (page 29), Greek Lamb-and-Pasta Stew (page 26), and Mexican Lime Soup (page 27), to name a few. Closer to home, we cover American regional specialties as well—from the politically correct Senatorial Bean Soup (page 32) to a Seafood-and-Sausage Gumbo (page 27) and New England Clam Chowder (page 28). No matter which recipe you make tonight, take comfort in this: You can't go wrong, because everyone loves a good bowl of soup.

Pour mixture into a large serving bowl; stir in remaining vegetable juice, 1 cup cucumber, and next 4 ingredients. Cover and chill at least 1 hour.

2. Spoon soup into bowls; garnish with cucumber slices and dill sprigs, if desired. Yield: 10 servings (serving size: 1 cup).

POINTS: 1; **Exchanges:** 3 Veg
Per serving: CAL 82 (10% from fat); PRO 3.8g; FAT 0.9g (sat 0.1g); CARB 16.3g; FIB 1.8g; CHOL 0mg; IRON 1.3mg; SOD 491mg; CALC 30mg

Greek Lamb-and-Pasta Stew

3 whole cloves
2 bay leaves
1 (3-inch) cinnamon stick
2 pounds lean, boned leg of lamb
Cooking spray
2 cups chopped onion
2 garlic cloves, minced
1 (14.5-ounce) can whole tomatoes, undrained and chopped
1 (14½-ounce) can beef broth
1 cup dry white wine
½ teaspoon salt
½ teaspoon dried rosemary
¼ teaspoon freshly ground pepper
3 cups hot cooked penne, without salt or fat (about 6 ounces uncooked tubular pasta)
1 cup (4 ounces) crumbled feta cheese, divided

1. Wrap cloves, bay leaves, and cinnamon stick in cheese cloth, and secure with string. Set spice pouch aside.

2. Trim fat from leg of lamb, and cut lamb into 1-inch cubes. Coat a Dutch oven with cooking spray, and place over medium-high heat until hot. Add half of lamb cubes, browning on all sides. Remove lamb from pan, reserving drippings in pan. Repeat procedure with remaining half of lamb. Set lamb aside.

3. Add onion and garlic to drippings in pan, and sauté until onion is tender. Return lamb to pan, and add spice pouch, tomatoes, and next 5 ingredients. Bring mixture to a boil; cover, reduce heat, and simmer 1 hour or until lamb is tender. Discard spice pouch.

4. Combine pasta and ⅔ cup cheese; toss gently.

Greek Lamb-and-Pasta Stew is garnished with a crumble of tangy feta cheese.

Garden Gazpacho

⅔ cup drained bottled roasted red bell peppers
1 teaspoon minced garlic
1 (46-ounce) can vegetable juice, divided
1 cup peeled seeded, finely chopped cucumber
1 cup finely chopped green bell pepper
1 tablespoon red wine vinegar
½ teaspoon pepper
1 (15-ounce) can chickpeas (garbanzo beans), drained
30 thin cucumber slices (optional)
Dill sprigs (optional)

1. Place roasted red bell peppers, garlic, and 1 cup vegetable juice in a blender; process until smooth.

Place ½ cup pasta in each of 6 shallow bowls; add 1 cup stew to each bowl. Sprinkle remaining cheese evenly over each serving. Yield: 6 servings.

POINTS: 8; **Exchanges:** 4½ Lean Meat, 1½ Starch, 1½ Veg
Per serving: CAL 391 (27% from fat); PRO 40.1g; FAT 11.6g (sat 5.4g); CARB 30.2g; FIB 2.8g; CHOL 114g; IRON 4.9mg; SOD 798mg; CALC 148mg

Seafood-and-Sausage Gumbo

⅓ cup all-purpose flour
1 (12-ounce) container standard oysters, undrained
Cooking spray
2 cups frozen cut okra
2 cups chopped onion
1½ cups diced green bell pepper
1½ cups diced celery
2 garlic cloves, crushed
⅔ cup water
¼ cup chopped fresh parsley
2½ teaspoons paprika
¾ teaspoon dried thyme
½ teaspoon dried oregano
½ teaspoon white pepper
½ teaspoon ground red pepper
½ teaspoon black pepper
¼ teaspoon salt
½ pound smoked turkey sausage, cut into ¼-inch slices
2 (8-ounce) bottles clam juice
1 (14½-ounce) can no-salt-added whole tomatoes, undrained and chopped
1 (14¼-ounce) can fat-free chicken broth
2 small bay leaves
1 pound small shrimp, peeled and deveined
½ pound lump crabmeat, drained and shell pieces removed
6 cups hot cooked long-grain rice, without salt or fat

1. Preheat oven to 350°.

2. Spread flour in bottom of a baking pan. Bake at 350° for 1 hour or until very brown, stirring every 15 minutes. Set browned flour aside.

3. Drain oysters, reserving liquid. Cover oysters, and chill. Set reserved oyster liquid aside.

4. Coat a Dutch oven with cooking spray; place over medium heat until hot. Add okra and next 4 ingredients; sauté 12 minutes or until tender. Stir in browned flour. Add reserved oyster liquid, water, and next 13 ingredients; bring to a boil, stirring constantly. Reduce heat, and simmer, uncovered, 1 hour.

5. Stir in oysters, shrimp, and crabmeat. Cover and simmer 10 minutes or until shrimp are done and edges of oysters begin to curl. Discard bay leaves. Serve gumbo over rice. Yield: 12 servings (serving size: 1 cup gumbo and ½ cup rice).

POINTS: 6; **Exchanges:** 2 Starch, 1½ Lean Meat, 1 Veg
Per serving: CAL 274 (20% from fat); PRO 18.1g; FAT 6.1g (sat 1.3g); CARB 35.6g; FIB 2g; CHOL 79mg; IRON 5.1mg; SOD 435mg; CALC 125mg

Mexican Lime Soup

This south-of-the-border soup comes complete with its own crunchy strips of fried corn tortillas.

2 (14½-ounce) cans chicken broth
1 medium onion, thinly sliced and separated into rings
1 large green bell pepper, cut into very thin strips
1 large red bell pepper, cut into very thin strips
⅔ cup thinly sliced carrot
⅔ cup sliced celery
½ teaspoon salt
¼ teaspoon pepper
1 cup shredded cooked chicken breast (about 5 ounces)
2 tablespoons chopped fresh cilantro
2 tablespoons fresh lime juice
Fried Corn Tortilla Strips
Lime slices (optional)

Made the healthy way, Seafood-and-Sausage Gumbo substitutes oven-browned flour for high-fat roux.

1. Combine first 8 ingredients in a large saucepan; bring to a boil. Cover, reduce heat, and simmer 10 minutes. Stir in chicken, cilantro, and lime juice; cook until thoroughly heated.

2. Spoon 1 cup soup into each of 7 bowls, and top evenly with Fried Corn Tortilla Strips. Garnish with lime slices, if desired. Yield: 7 servings.

POINTS: 2; **Exchanges:** 1 Veg, 1 Very Lean Meat, ½ Starch, ½ Fat **Per serving:** CAL 122 (29% from fat); PRO 10.1g; FAT 3.9g (sat 0.8g); CARB 11.9g; FIB 2g; CHOL 17mg; IRON 1.1mg; SOD 594mg; CALC 46mg

Fried Corn Tortilla Strips:

4   (6-inch) corn tortillas
1   tablespoon vegetable oil

1. Cut each tortilla into thin strips.

2. Heat oil in a nonstick skillet over medium-high heat until hot. Add tortilla strips; cook 3 minutes or until crisp, stirring occasionally. Remove tortilla strips from skillet with a slotted spoon; drain tortilla strips on paper towels. Yield: 1½ cups.

New England Clam Chowder

Look for bottled clam juice in supermarkets on the aisle with canned fish.

2   (6½-ounce) cans minced clams, undrained
Cooking spray
1   cup chopped onion
2   turkey-bacon slices
1   garlic clove, minced
3   cups peeled chopped red potato (about 1¼ pounds)
½   teaspoon dried thyme
2   (8-ounce) bottles clam juice
¼   cup plus 2 tablespoons all-purpose flour
2½ cups 2% reduced-fat milk
Freshly ground pepper (optional)
Chopped fresh parsley (optional)

1. Drain clams, reserving liquid; set both aside.

2. Coat a Dutch oven with cooking spray; place over medium heat until hot. Add onion, turkey-bacon, and garlic; sauté 5 minutes. Add reserved clam liquid, potato, thyme, and bottled clam juice; bring to a boil. Cover, reduce heat, and simmer 20 minutes or until potato is tender.

3. Place 2 cups potato mixture, including bacon,

in container of a blender; process until smooth. Return puréed potato mixture to chowder in pan; stir well. Stir in clams. Place flour in a small bowl; gradually add milk, stirring with a whisk until blended. Add flour mixture to chowder; cook over medium heat 10 minutes or until thick, stirring constantly. Spoon into bowls; sprinkle with freshly ground pepper, and garnish with parsley, if desired. Yield: 8 servings (serving size: 1 cup).

POINTS: 3; **Exchanges:** 1 Starch, ½ L-F Milk, ½ Very Lean Meat **Per serving:** CAL 164 (20% from fat); PRO 9.7g; FAT 3.7g (sat 1.5g); CARB 21.9g; FIB 1.5g; CHOL 27mg; IRON 2.5mg; SOD 564mg; CALC 133mg

Chile-Cheese Soup

2   dried pasilla chiles, halved lengthwise and seeded
4   large yellow bell peppers
1   large red bell pepper
2   teaspoons vegetable oil
1   cup chopped onion
2   garlic cloves, chopped
3   cups low-salt chicken broth
2½ cups peeled diced baking potato (about 1 pound)
1   cup diced carrot
½   teaspoon salt
¼   teaspoon white pepper
2   tablespoons plain low-fat yogurt
7   tablespoons (1¾ ounces) shredded Monterey Jack cheese

1. Combine chile halves and 1 cup water in a saucepan; bring to a boil. Remove from heat; cover and let stand 1 hour. Drain; finely chop chiles. Set aside.

2. Cut bell peppers in half lengthwise; discard stems, seeds, and membranes. Place pepper halves, skin side up, on a foil-lined baking sheet; flatten with hand. Broil 10 minutes or until blackened. Place peppers in a large zip-top plastic bag; seal. Let stand 15 minutes; peel.

3. Heat oil in a Dutch oven over medium heat. Add onion and garlic, and sauté 7 minutes. Stir in yellow bell pepper, broth, and next 4 ingredients; bring to a boil. Cover, reduce heat, and simmer 35 minutes or until vegetables are tender.

4. Place half of soup in a blender or food processor, and process until smooth; pour into a bowl. Repeat procedure with other half of soup; stir in chopped chiles.

5. Place red bell pepper and yogurt in a blender or food processor; process until smooth.

6. Spoon soup into bowls; top with red bell pepper purée and cheese. Yield: 7 servings (serving size: 1 cup soup, 1 tablespoon red bell pepper purée, and 1 tablespoon cheese).

POINTS: 3; **Exchanges:** 2 Veg, 1 Starch, 1 Fat
Per serving: CAL 153 (30% from fat); PRO 5.9g; FAT 5.1g (sat 1.7g); CARB 23.3g; FIB 4.5g; CHOL 6mg; IRON 2.9mg; SOD 262mg; CALC 87mg

Soupe à l'Oignon (French Onion Soup)

Substitute no-salt-added beef broth for the wine in this recipe, if desired.

6   (½-inch-thick) slices thin French bread baguette
1   tablespoon margarine
Cooking spray
6   cups thinly sliced onion
½   teaspoon sugar
⅛   teaspoon pepper
3   tablespoons all-purpose flour
4   (14¼-ounce) cans fat-free beef broth
1   (10-ounce) can beef consommé, undiluted
½   cup dry white wine
1   tablespoon Worcestershire sauce
6   tablespoons (1½ ounces) shredded Gruyère cheese

1. Preheat oven to 375°.

2. Place bread slices on a baking sheet. Bake at 375° for 8 minutes or until lightly browned; set bread aside.

3. Melt margarine over medium-low heat in a Dutch oven coated with cooking spray. Add onion; sauté 5 minutes. Sprinkle sugar and pepper evenly over onion. Reduce heat to low, and cook 20 minutes or until onion is golden brown, stirring frequently.

4. Sprinkle flour evenly over onion, and cook 2 minutes, stirring constantly. Gradually add beef broth, consommé, and wine; bring to a boil. Par-tially cover, reduce heat, and simmer 30 minutes. Remove from heat; stir in Worcestershire sauce.

5. Spoon 1½ cups soup into each of 6 ovenproof soup bowls; top each serving with 1 bread slice and 1 tablespoon cheese. Place soup bowls on a large baking sheet, and broil 1 minute or until cheese melts. Yield: 6 servings.

POINTS: 4; **Exchanges:** 1½ Starch, 1 Veg, ½ Hi-Fat Meat
Per serving: CAL 204 (23% from fat); PRO 8g; FAT 5.1g (sat 1.9g); CARB 28.7g; FIB 3g; CHOL 8mg; IRON 1mg; SOD 522mg; CALC 113mg

Cold Fruit Soup

A splash of sweet white wine, such as Riesling or Gewürztraminer, enhances the flavors of this soup.

1   pound cooking apples, peeled, cored, and coarsely chopped
1   pound ripe pears, peeled, cored, and coarsely chopped

French Onion Soup is traditionally topped by slices of French bread toasted with Gruyère cheese.

Country-French Vegetable Soup

1   pound plums, pitted and coarsely chopped
2   cups water
½   cup fresh breadcrumbs
1   tablespoon grated lemon rind
1   tablespoon fresh lemon juice
½   teaspoon ground cinnamon
½   cup sugar
¼   cup seedless raspberry jam
1   cup cranberry juice cocktail
¾   cup sweet white wine

1. Combine first 8 ingredients in a large Dutch oven; bring to a boil. Cover, reduce heat, and simmer 20 minutes or until fruit is tender. Let cool slightly.

2. Place one-third of mixture in a blender or food processor; process until smooth. Pour puréed fruit mixture into a large bowl. Repeat procedure twice with remaining fruit mixture. Stir sugar and raspberry jam into warm puréed fruit mixture, stirring until sugar and jam dissolve. Stir in cranberry juice cocktail and wine. Cover and chill thoroughly. Yield: 8 servings (serving size: about 1 cup).

POINTS: 4; **Exchanges:** 3½ Fruit
Per serving: CAL 219 (4% from fat); PRO 1.1g; FAT 0.9g (sat 0.1g); CARB 51.7g; FIB 3.5g; CHOL 0mg; IRON 0.7mg; SOD 23mg; CALC 23mg

Country-French Vegetable Soup

2   teaspoons olive oil
2   cups chopped green cabbage
1   cup chopped onion
1   cup sliced carrot
1   cup sliced celery
1   cup diced red potato
1   teaspoon caraway seeds
1   cup water
2   (14½-ounce) cans vegetable broth (such as Swanson's)
1   cup drained canned cannellini beans or other white beans
2   tablespoons minced fresh parsley
2   teaspoons chopped fresh or ½ teaspoon dried dill
½   teaspoon pepper

1. Heat olive oil in a Dutch oven over medium-high heat. Add cabbage and next 5 ingredients;

sauté 2 minutes. Add water and vegetable broth; bring to a boil. Cover, reduce heat, and simmer 30 minutes. Add remaining ingredients, and cook until thoroughly heated. Yield: 4 servings (serving size: 1¾ cups).

POINTS: 3; **Exchanges:** 2 Starch, 1 Veg
Per serving: CAL 184 (20% from fat); PRO 5.7g; FAT 4.1g (sat 0.7g); CARB 33.1g; FIB 7.6g; CHOL 0mg; IRON 1.8mg; SOD 425mg; CALC 77mg

Split Pea Soup With Garlic Croutons

Homemade croutons add a garlicky crunch to this thick and hearty soup.

1   tablespoon vegetable oil
2   cups chopped carrot
1½   cups diced cooked ham
1   cup chopped onion
1   cup chopped celery
1   tablespoon minced garlic
¼   teaspoon ground red pepper
¼   teaspoon ground cloves
10   cups water
2   (14½-ounce) cans chicken broth
1   (16-ounce) package dried green split peas
1   teaspoon salt
½   teaspoon freshly ground pepper
1   bay leaf
Garlic Croutons

1. Heat oil in a Dutch oven over medium-high heat. Add carrot and next 3 ingredients; sauté until vegetables are tender. Stir in garlic, red pepper, and cloves; sauté 30 seconds. Stir in water and next 5 ingredients; bring to a boil. Cover, reduce heat, and simmer 1 hour, stirring occasionally. Remove from heat; let cool 5 minutes. Discard bay leaf.

2. Place half of soup in a blender or food processor, and process until smooth. Pour into a bowl. Repeat procedure with remaining soup. Stir well. Spoon soup into bowls; top with Garlic Croutons. Yield: 13 servings (serving size: 1 cup soup and about ⅓ cup croutons).

POINTS: 5; **Exchanges:** 2 Starch, 1½ Lean Meat
Per serving: CAL 251 (26% from fat); PRO 16g; FAT 7.2g (sat 1.5g); CARB 31.4g; FIB 3.5g; CHOL 15mg; IRON 2.4mg; SOD 574mg; CALC 47mg

Garlic Croutons:

6   (1-inch-thick) slices French bread, cubed
3   tablespoons olive oil
1   teaspoon minced garlic
½   teaspoon salt
½   teaspoon freshly ground pepper

1. Preheat oven to 425°.

2. Place bread cubes in a bowl. Combine oil and next 3 ingredients; drizzle over bread cubes, tossing well to coat. Spread cubes in a single layer on a jelly-roll pan. Bake at 425° for 8 minutes or until golden, stirring after 4 minutes. Yield: 4 cups.

Senatorial Bean Soup

For decades this soup has been served in the cafeteria of our nation's Capitol. If you prefer a smooth, creamy texture, purée all of the soup. It's even better when refrigerated several hours and then reheated.

1   cup dried navy beans
2   tablespoons margarine
Cooking spray
2½ cups chopped leek
2   cups sliced carrot
1   cup thinly sliced celery
1   cup diced lean smoked ham
4   garlic cloves, minced
8   cups water
2   teaspoons chicken-flavored bouillon
      granules
1   teaspoon beef-flavored bouillon granules
1   teaspoon rubbed sage
2   bay leaves
Celery leaves (optional)

1. Sort and wash beans; place in a large Dutch oven. Cover with water to 2 inches above beans; bring to a boil, and cook 2 minutes. Remove from heat; cover and let stand 1 hour. Drain beans in a colander; set aside.

2. Melt margarine over medium-high heat in Dutch oven coated with cooking spray. Add leek and next 4 ingredients; sauté 10 minutes. Add beans, 8 cups water, and next 4 ingredients; bring mixture to a boil. Cover, reduce heat, and simmer 1½ hours or until beans are very tender. Discard bay leaves.

3. Place half of soup in a blender or food processor; process until smooth. Return puréed bean mixture to soup in pan; cook over medium-low heat 30 minutes. Spoon soup into bowls; garnish with celery leaves, if desired. Yield: 8 servings (serving size: 1 cup).

POINTS: 3; **Exchanges:** 2 Veg, 1 Starch, ½ Very Lean Meat, ½ Fat **Per serving:** CAL 174 (24% from fat); PRO 10g; FAT 4.7g (sat 1.1g); CARB 24.5g; FIB 4g; CHOL 9mg; IRON 2.5mg; SOD 525mg; CALC 77mg

Pork Goulash

1   (3-pound) lean, boned pork loin roast
Cooking spray
2   bacon slices, chopped
1   cup diced onion
½   cup sliced carrot
½   cup sliced parsnip
1   cup tomato juice
1   cup beef broth
1   tablespoon brown sugar
2   teaspoons paprika
1   teaspoon salt
1   teaspoon dried marjoram
½   teaspoon pepper
1   (12-ounce) can light beer
6   cups coarsely chopped Savoy or green
      cabbage
3   cups peeled cubed baking potato

1. Trim fat from pork; cut pork into 1-inch pieces. Coat a Dutch oven with cooking spray; place over medium-high heat until hot. Add pork; cook 5 minutes, browning on all sides. Drain in a colander; set aside.

2. Cook bacon in Dutch oven over medium heat until crisp. Add onion, carrot, and parsnip to pan; sauté 10 minutes or until tender. Add pork, tomato juice, and next 7 ingredients; bring to a boil. Cover, reduce heat, and simmer 1½ hours or until pork is tender, stirring occasionally. Add cabbage and potato; cover and simmer 30 minutes or until potato is tender. Yield: 8 servings (serving size: 1¼ cups).

POINTS: 7; **Exchanges:** 2 Veg, 1 Starch, 3½ Lean Meat **Per serving:** CAL 325 (30% from fat); PRO 31.2g; FAT 10.9g (sat 3.7g); CARB 23.3g; FIB 2.5g; CHOL 84mg; IRON 2.2mg; SOD 749mg; CALC 51mg

Asian Chicken-Vegetable Soup

This hearty broth teems with traditional Asian ingredients.

6   cups chicken broth
1   tablespoon soy sauce
1   teaspoon sugar
⅛   teaspoon dark sesame oil
3   tablespoons cornstarch
¼   cup water
1   cup thinly sliced cooked chicken breast
1   cup sliced bok choy
1   cup sliced fresh mushrooms
½   cup drained canned sliced bamboo shoots
½   cup drained canned sliced water chestnuts
¼   pound fresh snow peas, trimmed and cut into 1-inch pieces
1   cup frozen cooked peeled small shrimp, thawed
½   cup chow mein noodles

1. Combine first 4 ingredients in a Dutch oven. Place over medium heat, and cook 15 minutes or until thoroughly heated.

2. Combine cornstarch and water, stirring until well blended. Gradually add cornstarch mixture to broth mixture, stirring well. Cook until mixture is slightly thick and bubbly, stirring constantly. Reduce heat to medium low; add sliced chicken breast and next 4 ingredients, and cook 5 minutes. Add snow peas and shrimp; cook an additional 1 minute. Spoon soup into bowls, and top with chow mein noodles. Yield: 8 servings (servings size: 1 cup soup and 1 tablespoon chow mein noodles).

POINTS: 2; **Exchanges**: 1½ Very Lean Meat, 1 Veg, ½ Starch
Per serving: CAL 123 (21% from fat); PRO 13.8g; FAT 2.9g (sat 0.7g); CARB 9g; FIB 1.4g; CHOL 41mg; IRON 1.8mg; SOD 882mg; CALC 36mg

Roasted Garlic-Potato Soup

This rich soup gets its hearty flavor from bacon and garlic.

5   whole garlic heads
2   bacon slices, diced
1   cup diced onion
1   cup diced carrot
2   garlic cloves, minced
6   cups peeled diced baking potato (about 2 pounds)

4   cups low-salt chicken broth
½   teaspoon salt
¼   teaspoon pepper
1   bay leaf
1   cup 2% reduced-fat milk
¼   cup chopped fresh parsley

1. Preheat oven to 350°.

2. Remove white papery skin from garlic heads (do not peel or separate cloves); cut off top one-third of each garlic head. Wrap each head separately in foil. Bake at 350° for 1 hour or until garlic is soft. Let cool 10 minutes. Squeeze garlic heads to extract ¼ cup garlic pulp, and set aside. Discard skins.

3. Cook bacon in a large saucepan over medium-high heat until crisp. Add onion, carrot, and minced garlic; sauté 5 minutes. Add potato and

Asian Chicken-Vegetable Soup brims with crunchy bamboo shoots, water chestnuts, and snow peas; each serving gets extra snap from a sprinkling of chow mein noodles.

next 4 ingredients; bring to a boil. Cover, reduce heat, and simmer 20 minutes or until potato is tender. Discard bay leaf.

4. Place garlic pulp and 2 cups potato mixture in a blender or food processor, and process until mixture is smooth. Return purée to potato mixture in pan; stir in milk, and cook over low heat until thoroughly heated. Remove from heat, and stir in chopped parsley. Yield: 7 servings (serving size: 1 cup).

POINTS: 3; **Exchanges:** 2 Starch, ½ Sk Milk
Per serving: CAL 199 (14% from fat); PRO 7.8g; FAT 3g (sat 1.1g); CARB 38g; FIB 3.9g; CHOL 5mg; IRON 2.8mg; SOD 300mg; CALC 150mg

Chicken Ragout With Pumpkin Dumplings revisits the German delicacy spaetzle with fall's favorite vegetable.

Chicken Ragout With Pumpkin Dumplings

If desired, you can substitute the same amount of unsweetened canned pumpkin for the fresh pumpkin.

1   teaspoon dried thyme
¾   teaspoon freshly ground pepper, divided
4   skinned, boned chicken breast halves (about ¾ pound)
7   skinned, boned chicken thighs (about ¾ pound)
1   tablespoon vegetable oil
1   (1-pound) package frozen small white onions
6   cups sliced fresh shiitake mushroom caps (about 1 pound)
3   cups low-salt chicken broth, divided
½   cup dry white wine
2   garlic cloves, minced
1¼ cups all-purpose flour, divided
1   teaspoon salt, divided
2   tablespoons minced fresh parsley, divided
1   teaspoon baking powder
½   teaspoon baking soda
1½ tablespoons vegetable shortening
½   cup mashed cooked fresh pumpkin
½   cup low-fat buttermilk
1   cup fat-free sour cream

1. Sprinkle thyme and ½ teaspoon pepper over chicken pieces. Heat vegetable oil in a large Dutch oven over medium-high heat. Add chicken; cook 5 minutes on each side or until browned. Remove chicken from pan; set aside.

2. Add onions to drippings in pan; sauté 5 minutes or until lightly browned. Remove onions from pan; set aside.

3. Add mushroom caps and ¼ cup chicken broth to pan, and cook 3 minutes or until liquid evaporates, stirring constantly. Return chicken and onions to pan. Add 2½ cups chicken broth, wine, and garlic; bring to a boil. Reduce heat, and simmer 1 minute.

4. Place ¼ cup flour and ½ teaspoon salt in a small bowl; gradually add remaining ¼ cup chicken broth, stirring with a whisk until mixture is well blended. Add flour mixture to pan,

stirring well. Cover and simmer 20 minutes, stirring occasionally.

5. Combine remaining 1 cup flour, remaining ¼ teaspoon pepper, remaining ½ teaspoon salt, 1 tablespoon parsley, baking powder, and baking soda in a medium bowl; cut in shortening with a pastry blender or 2 knives until mixture resembles coarse meal. Add pumpkin and low-fat buttermilk to flour mixture, stirring just until moist; set dough aside.

6. Stir sour cream into chicken mixture. Drop dough onto chicken mixture to form 6 dumplings. Cover and simmer 20 minutes (do not boil or sour cream will curdle). Remove from heat, and spoon into 6 individual serving bowls. Sprinkle remaining 1 tablespoon parsley evenly over each serving. Yield: 6 servings (serving size: 3 ounces chicken, ¾ cup sauce, 1 dumpling, and ½ teaspoon parsley).

POINTS: 8; **Exchanges:** 4 Very Lean Meat, 2 Starch, 1 Veg, 1 Fat **Per serving:** CAL 372 (23% from fat); PRO 34.1g; FAT 9.5g (sat 2.5g); CARB 36.9g; FIB 2g; CHOL 80mg; IRON 4.4mg; SOD 672mg; CALC 106mg

Oyster-Artichoke Soup

1   (16-ounce) container standard oysters, undrained
1   teaspoon butter or margarine
½   cup chopped green onions
3   (8-ounce) bottles clam juice
1   tablespoon chopped fresh parsley
½   teaspoon dried thyme
¼   teaspoon ground red pepper
¼   cup plus 2 tablespoons all-purpose flour
2   cups 2% reduced-fat milk
1   (14-ounce) can quartered artichoke hearts, drained
Freshly ground pepper (optional)
Sliced green onions (optional)

1. Drain oysters, reserving ¼ cup juice, and set both aside.

2. Melt butter in a large saucepan. Add chopped green onions, and sauté 3 minutes. Add reserved ¼ cup oyster juice, clam juice, and next 3 ingredients; bring mixture to a boil. Reduce heat, and simmer 10 minutes.

3. Place flour in a small bowl; gradually add milk, stirring with a whisk until blended. Add milk mixture to soup; cook over medium heat 6 minutes or until thick, stirring constantly. Stir in oysters and artichokes; cook an additional 3 minutes or until edges of oysters curl.

4. Spoon soup into bowls; sprinkle with freshly ground pepper, and garnish with sliced green onions, if desired. Yield: 7 servings (serving size: 1 cup).

POINTS: 3; **Exchanges:** ½ Starch, ½ L-F Milk, ½ Very Lean Meat **Per serving:** CAL 127 (26% from fat); PRO 8.9g ; FAT 3.7g (sat 1.4g); CARB 14.8g; FIB 0.7g; CHOL 41mg; IRON 5.3mg; SOD 443mg; CALC 149mg

Lamb-and-Black Bean Chili

You can substitute lean ground beef for ground lamb, if desired.

1½   pounds lean ground lamb
1   cup chopped onion
2   garlic cloves, minced
2   (14½-ounce) cans no-salt-added whole tomatoes, undrained and chopped
1   cup dry red wine
1   tablespoon chili powder
1½   teaspoons ground cumin
1½   teaspoons dried oregano

Serve Oyster-Artichoke Soup as an elegantly creamy first course.

1   teaspoon sugar
¼   teaspoon salt
3   (15-ounce) cans black beans, drained
¼   teaspoon hot sauce

1. Combine lamb, onion, and garlic in a Dutch oven; cook over medium heat until lamb is browned, stirring to crumble. Drain in a colander, and set aside. Wipe drippings from pan with a paper towel. Return meat mixture to pan. Stir in tomatoes and next 6 ingredients; bring to a boil. Cover, reduce heat, and simmer 2 hours, stirring occasionally. Stir in beans and hot sauce. Cover and simmer 30 minutes. Yield: 8 servings (serving size: 1 cup).

POINTS: 6; **Exchanges:** 3 Lean Meat, 2 Starch
Per serving: CAL 311 (20% from fat); PRO 27.9g; FAT 6.9g (sat 2.3g); CARB 30.8g; FIB 5.6g; CHOL 57mg; IRON 4.5mg; SOD 413mg; CALC 91mg

White Bean Chili

For variety, substitute fresh ground turkey for the chicken in this chili.

1   pound dried Great Northern beans
1   tablespoon olive oil
2   medium onions, chopped
2   teaspoons ground cumin
1½ teaspoons dried oregano
Dash of ground red pepper
2   (4.5-ounce) cans chopped green chiles, undrained
4   garlic cloves, minced
6   cups chicken broth
5   cups chopped cooked chicken breast (about 1½ pounds)
3   cups (12 ounces) shredded Monterey Jack cheese, divided
½   teaspoon salt
½   teaspoon pepper
¾   cup sour cream
¾   cup salsa
Chopped fresh parsley (optional)

1. Sort and wash beans; place in a large ovenproof Dutch oven. Cover with water to 2 inches above beans; cover and let stand 8 hours. Drain in a colander; set beans aside.

2. Heat oil in Dutch oven over medium-high heat. Add onions; sauté until tender. Add cumin

and next 4 ingredients; sauté 2 minutes. Add beans and chicken broth; bring to a boil. Cover, reduce heat, and simmer 2 hours or until beans are tender, stirring occasionally. Add chicken, 1 cup cheese, salt and pepper; bring to a boil. Reduce heat, and simmer, uncovered, 10 minutes, stirring frequently.

3. Spoon chili into bowls; top with remaining cheese, sour cream, and salsa. Yield: 12 servings (serving size: 1 cup chili, about 2½ tablespoons cheese, 1 tablespoon sour cream, and 1 tablespoon salsa).

POINTS: 7; **Exchanges:** 2 Starch, 4 Lean Meat, ½ Fat
Per serving: CAL 404 (28% from fat); PRO 34.7g; FAT 12.7g (sat 5.8g); CARB 30.6g; FIB 8.4g; CHOL 83.2mg; IRON 3.2mg; SOD 948mg; CALC 293mg

Beef Burgundy Stew

For a nonalcoholic version of this stew, use the following to replace the 3 cups dry red wine: 1 (14¼-ounce) can fat-free beef broth, ⅔ cup non-alcoholic red wine, ⅓ cup water, and ¼ cup red wine vinegar.

1½ pounds lean, boned round steak (about ½ inch thick)
Cooking spray
1   teaspoon vegetable oil
½   teaspoon dried thyme
2   large garlic cloves, minced
2   bay leaves
3   cups dry red wine
¼   cup tomato paste
2½ cups quartered fresh mushrooms (about ½ pound)
½   cup water
12   small red potatoes, quartered (about 1½ pounds)
6   medium carrots, cut into 1-inch pieces (about 1 pound)
2   small onions, peeled and quartered (about ½ pound)
2   (10½-ounce) cans low-salt chicken broth
3   tablespoons cornstarch
3   tablespoons water
¼   cup chopped fresh parsley
1¼ teaspoons salt
¼   teaspoon pepper

1. Trim fat from steak; cut steak into 1-inch cubes. Coat a Dutch oven with cooking spray;

EDITOR'S CHOICE

add oil, and place over medium-high heat until hot. Add steak, browning on all sides. Drain steak in a colander. Wipe drippings from pan with a paper towel.

2. Return steak to pan; add thyme, garlic, and bay leaves. Place over medium heat, and cook 1 minute. Add wine and tomato paste; bring to a boil. Cover, reduce heat, and simmer 1½ hours or until steak is tender. Add mushrooms and next 5 ingredients; bring to a boil. Cover, reduce heat, and simmer 40 minutes or until vegetables are tender. Discard bay leaves.

3. Combine cornstarch and 3 tablespoons water in a small bowl; stir well. Add to stew, and cook 2 minutes or until mixture is thick, stirring constantly. Remove from heat; stir in chopped parsley, salt, and pepper. Yield: 12 servings (serving size: 1 cup).

POINTS: 4; **Exchanges:** 1½ Starch, 2 Med-fat Meat
Per serving: CAL 220 (15% from fat); PRO 16.8g; FAT 3.7g (sat 1.1g); CARB 20.9g; FIB 3.1g; CHOL 36mg; IRON 3.4mg; SOD 312mg; CALC 36mg

Chicken Noodle Soup

Make double batches of the broth for this soup and freeze it for later use.

13 cups water
1 tablespoon black peppercorns
1 teaspoon dried basil
1 teaspoon dried oregano
3¾ pounds chicken pieces (white and dark meat), skinned
3 medium parsnips or carrots, each scraped and quartered
3 garlic cloves, halved
2 medium leeks or onions, each trimmed and quartered
2 stalks celery, each quartered
2 cups sliced carrot
¾ teaspoon salt
⅛ teaspoon pepper
1½ cups uncooked fine or medium egg noodles

1. Combine first 9 ingredients in an 8-quart Dutch oven or stockpot; bring to a boil. Reduce heat to medium, and cook, uncovered, 1 hour. Remove from heat.

2. Remove chicken pieces from broth; place chicken in a bowl, and chill 15 minutes. Strain broth through a sieve into a large bowl, and discard solids.

3. Remove chicken from bones, and shred meat into bite-size pieces. Discard bones. Return reserved broth to pan. Add shredded chicken, sliced carrot, salt, and pepper, and bring mixture to a boil. Partially cover, reduce heat to medium, and cook 10 minutes, stirring occasionally. Add egg noodles; partially cover, and cook an additional 10 minutes. Yield: 7 servings (serving size: 1½ cups).

POINTS: 5; **Exchanges:** 4 Very Lean Meat, 1 Veg, ½ Starch, ½ Fat
Per serving: CAL 227 (18% from fat); PRO 33.3g; FAT 4.6g (sat 1.2g); CARB 11.1g; FIB 1.3g; CHOL 111mg; IRON 1.9mg; SOD 374mg; CALC 31mg

Chicken Noodle Soup may or may not cure a cold, but it does make a body feel good.

Top-Rated Sides and Salads

VIBRANT COLOR AND FLAVOR MOVE THESE
SIDE DISHES FRONT AND CENTER.

A*lthough the recipes in this chapter are officially classified as side dishes,*
some of them are delicious enough that you'll want to make entire

meals out of them. In fact, even when served as a side dish, many of these

recipes can transform simple grilled or poached fish, chicken, or beef into a

spectacular meal, simply by appearing on the same plate. Why serve steamed

vegetables and boiled rice when, with a little more effort, you can enjoy

Tangy Marinated *Fresh Tomato-Squash Salad (page 49) and Herbed Basmati Rice (page 41).*
Coleslaw gets its
kick from a cider *From weeknight meals to fabulous weekend feasts, make every meal count for*
vinaigrette spiked
with horseradish. *more with these starring side dishes.*

Herbed Basmati Rice

Tangy Marinated Coleslaw

4 cups thinly sliced green cabbage
1½ cups seeded sliced cucumber
1 cup coarsely shredded carrot
½ cup diced red onion
½ cup diced green bell pepper
¼ cup cider vinegar
1 tablespoon sugar
1 tablespoon Dijon mustard
1 tablespoon vegetable oil
2 teaspoons prepared horseradish
½ teaspoon pepper
¼ teaspoon salt
Cucumber slices (optional)

1. Combine first 5 ingredients in a large bowl; toss well.

2. Combine vinegar and next 6 ingredients in a bowl; stir well with a whisk. Pour over slaw; toss gently. Cover and chill 8 hours. Garnish with cucumber slices, if desired. Yield: 6 servings (serving size: 1 cup).

POINTS: 1; Exchanges: 2 Veg, ½ Fat
Per serving: CAL 64 (38% from fat); PRO 1.3g; FAT 2.7g (sat 0.5g); CARB 9.8g; FIB 2.5g; CHOL 0mg; IRON 0.8mg; SOD 189mg; CALC 39mg

Chilled Broccoli-Pasta Salad

3 cups small fresh broccoli florets
3 cups cooked rotini (about 6 ounces uncooked corkscrew pasta), without salt or fat
1 cup thinly sliced red cabbage
1 garlic clove, peeled
3 tablespoons white wine vinegar
3 tablespoons mango chutney
1 tablespoon Dijon mustard
2 teaspoons sugar
¼ teaspoon pepper
2 tablespoons vegetable oil

1. Drop broccoli into a large saucepan of boiling water, and return to a boil. Cook 1 minute, and drain. Pour cold water over broccoli, and drain. Combine broccoli, pasta, and cabbage in a large bowl; set aside.

2. Place garlic in a blender; process until minced. Add vinegar and next 4 ingredients; process until smooth. With blender on, add oil through open-ing in lid; process until blended. Pour over pasta mixture; toss gently. Cover and chill 30 minutes. Yield: 5 servings (serving size: 1 cup).

POINTS: 4; Exchanges: 1½ Starch, 1 Veg, 1 Fat
Per serving: CAL 193 (29% from fat); PRO 4.9g; FAT 6.3g (sat 1.1g); CARB 29.9g; FIB 3g; CHOL 0mg; IRON 1.6mg; SOD 127mg; CALC 41mg

Herbed Basmati Rice

1 tablespoon margarine
1 large garlic clove, minced
¾ cup uncooked basmati rice
1½ cups water
½ teaspoon salt
3 tablespoons thinly sliced green onion tops
1 tablespoon minced fresh basil
1½ teaspoons minced fresh thyme
3 tablespoons (¾ ounce) grated fresh Parmesan cheese
Thyme sprigs (optional)

1. Melt margarine in a small saucepan over medium-high heat. Add garlic; sauté 1 minute. Stir in rice. Add water and salt; bring to a boil. Cover, reduce heat, and simmer 20 minutes or until rice is tender and liquid is absorbed. Stir in green onion tops, basil, and thyme. Spoon into a serving bowl; sprinkle with Parmesan cheese. Garnish with thyme sprigs, if desired. Yield: 4 servings (serving size: ¾ cup).

POINTS: 4; Exchanges: 2 Starch, ½ Fat
Per serving: CAL 196 (27% from fat); PRO 6.4g; FAT 5.8g (sat 2.4g); CARB 28.5g; FIB 0.5g; CHOL 7mg; IRON 1.7mg; SOD 499mg; CALC 142mg

Portuguese Cucumber Salad

2 cups seeded diced cucumber
½ teaspoon salt
2 red bell peppers
4 plum tomatoes, cut in half lengthwise
2 tablespoons minced fresh cilantro
2½ tablespoons red wine vinegar
1 tablespoon extra-virgin olive oil
¼ teaspoon freshly ground pepper
2 garlic cloves, minced

1. Combine cucumber and salt in a medium bowl; toss well. Let stand 30 minutes; drain. Place cucumber on several layers of paper towels; pat gently to remove excess moisture.

2. Cut bell peppers in half lengthwise; discard stems, seeds, and membranes. Place bell pepper halves and tomatoes, skin sides up, on a foil-lined baking sheet; flatten peppers with hand. Broil 15 minutes or until blackened. Place peppers and tomatoes in a zip-top plastic bag; seal bag, and let stand 5 minutes. Peel and dice peppers and tomatoes; place in a large bowl. Stir in cucumber, cilantro, and remaining ingredients. Cover and chill. Yield: 12 servings (serving size: ½ cup).

POINTS: 0; **Exchanges:** 1 Free
Per serving: CAL 21 (56% from fat); PRO 0.5g; FAT 1.3g (sat 0.2g); CARB 2.4g; FIB 0.7g; CHOL 0mg; IRON 0.4mg; SOD 101mg; CALC 6mg

Creamed Spinach

2   (10-ounce) bags fresh spinach
Cooking spray
2   tablespoons minced shallots
2   teaspoons all-purpose flour
⅛   teaspoon salt
⅛   teaspoon ground nutmeg
½   cup skim milk
½   cup tub-style light cream cheese, softened

1. Remove large stems from spinach; rinse spinach under cold water, and drain. Place spinach in a large Dutch oven (spinach will be tightly packed); cover and cook over medium heat 5 minutes or until spinach wilts, stirring well after 2 minutes. Drain spinach in a colander, pressing spinach with the back of a spoon to remove as much moisture as possible.

2. Coat Dutch oven with cooking spray, and place over medium heat until hot. Add shallots; sauté 2 minutes. Combine flour, salt, and nutmeg; add to shallots, and cook 30 seconds, stirring constantly. Add milk and cream cheese, and cook 1 minute or until thick, stirring with a whisk until blended. Stir in spinach; cook 30 seconds or until thoroughly heated. Yield: 4 servings (serving size: ⅔ cup).

POINTS: 1; **Exchanges:** 2 Veg, 1 Fat, ½ Very Lean Meat
Per serving: CAL 110 (44% from fat); PRO 7.9g; FAT 5.4g (sat 3g); CARB 9.5g; FIB 5.2g; CHOL 17mg; IRON 3.6mg; SOD 346mg; CALC 204mg

Tomatoes Vinaigrette

⅓   cup water
3   tablespoons cider vinegar
1   tablespoon chopped red onion
¼   teaspoon ground coriander
⅛   teaspoon sugar
⅛   teaspoon dry mustard
⅛   teaspoon paprika
Dash of chili powder
Dash of garlic powder
2   medium tomatoes, cut into
     ¼-inch-thick slices
Curly leaf lettuce leaves (optional)

1. Combine first 9 ingredients in an 11- x 7-inch baking dish; stir well. Add tomato slices, turning to coat. Cover; let stand at room temperature at least 30 minutes. Serve tomato slices on lettuce-lined salad plates, if desired. Yield: 4 servings.

POINTS: 0; **Exchanges:** 1 Free
Per serving: CAL 17 (11% from fat); PRO 0.6g; FAT 0.2g (sat 0g); CARB 4g; FIB 0.9g; CHOL 0mg; IRON 0.4mg; SOD 6mg; CALC 5mg

Classic Potato Salad

1½   pounds baking potatoes, halved
½   cup finely chopped red onion
¼   cup finely chopped celery
¼   cup sweet pickle relish
2   hard-cooked large eggs, coarsely chopped
⅓   cup light mayonnaise
2   tablespoons cider vinegar
1   tablespoon Dijon mustard
¼   teaspoon salt
¼   teaspoon pepper

1. Cook potato halves in boiling water 25 minutes or until potatoes are tender; drain and let cool completely.

2. Cut potatoes into ½-inch cubes. Combine potatoes, onion, celery, relish, and eggs in a large bowl. Combine mayonnaise and next 4 ingredients in a small bowl; stir with a whisk. Pour dressing over potato salad; toss gently to coat. Cover and chill at least 8 hours. Yield: 6 servings (serving size: ¾ cup).

POINTS: 4; **Exchanges:** 2½ Starch, ½ Fat
Per serving: CAL 208 (25% from fat); PRO 5g; FAT 5.7g (sat 1.1g); CARB 35.1g; FIB 2.4g; CHOL 75mg; IRON 1.9mg; SOD 387mg; CALC 26mg

Tomatoes Vinaigrette

3. Place flour in a medium saucepan; gradually add remaining ¼ cup milk, stirring with a whisk until blended. Stir in strained milk mixture; cook over medium-low heat 3 minutes or until thick, stirring constantly. Stir in corn mixture and salt; cook over medium-low heat 15 minutes or until corn is tender, stirring frequently. Sprinkle with coarsely ground pepper, if desired. Yield: 6 servings (serving size: ½ cup).

POINTS: 2; **Exchanges:** 1½ Starch
Per serving: CAL 114 (17% from fat); PRO 4.8g; FAT 2.2g (sat 1.1g); CARB 20.4g; FIB 2g; CHOL 7mg; IRON 0.6mg; SOD 245mg; CALC 102mg

Roasted Sweet Potato Wedges

2   (8-ounce) sweet potatoes
1   teaspoon olive oil
½   teaspoon curry powder
¼   teaspoon salt
¼   teaspoon ground cumin
⅛   teaspoon ground cloves
⅛   teaspoon pepper

1. Preheat oven to 425°.
2. Peel sweet potatoes; cut each potato lengthwise into 12 wedges. Combine sweet potato wedges and remaining ingredients in a large bowl; toss gently to coat. Place wedges in a single layer on a baking sheet; bake at 425° for 25 minutes or until very tender. Yield: 4 servings (serving size: 6 wedges).

POINTS: 2; **Exchanges:** 1½ Starch
Per serving: CAL 101 (13% from fat); PRO 1.5g; FAT 1.5g (sat 0.2g); CARB 20.9g; FIB 2.7g; CHOL 0mg; IRON 0.7mg; SOD 158mg; CALC 22mg

Citrus Salad With Lime Vinaigrette

Four lettuces—Boston, Bibb, red leaf, and romaine—add flavor, texture, and color to this refreshing citrus salad. You may use 4 cups of one lettuce, if desired.

2   tablespoons fresh lime juice
2   teaspoons rice vinegar
2   teaspoons honey
2   teaspoons vegetable oil
½   teaspoon salt
¼   teaspoon ground ginger

Creamed Corn, made from fresh-shucked ears, is a rich, creamy side dish best served in summer.

Creamed Corn

4   ears fresh corn, shucked
1   cup 2% reduced-fat milk, divided
¾   cup coarsely chopped onion
½   teaspoon black peppercorns
¼   cup all-purpose flour
½   teaspoon salt
Coarsely ground pepper (optional)

1. Working over a large bowl, cut off tops of corn kernels, and scrape "milk" and any remaining pulp from cobs using the dull side of a knife blade. Set corn mixture aside, and reserve 1 cob (discard remaining 3 cobs).
2. Cut reserved cob in half. Combine cob halves, ¾ cups milk, onion, and peppercorns in a medium saucepan; bring to a boil over medium heat. Reduce heat, and simmer, uncovered, 5 minutes, stirring occasionally. Strain milk mixture; discard cob halves, onion, and peppercorns.

⅛ teaspoon ground red pepper
1 cup torn Boston lettuce
1 cup torn Bibb lettuce
1 cup torn red leaf lettuce
1 cup torn romaine lettuce
1 navel orange, peeled and sectioned
1 grapefruit, peeled and sectioned
1 small red onion, thinly sliced and
  separated into rings

1. Combine first 7 ingredients; stir well.

2. Combine lettuces in a large bowl; toss gently.
Arrange 1 cup lettuce on each of 4 salad plates;
top evenly with orange sections, grapefruit sections, and onion rings. Drizzle evenly with vinaigrette. Yield: 4 servings.

POINTS: 1; **Exchanges:** ½ Fruit, 2 Veg, ½ Fat
Per serving: CAL 92 (25% from fat); PRO 2.1g; FAT 2.6g (sat 0.4g);
CARB 17.1g; FIB 3.8g; CHOL 0mg; IRON 0.8mg; SOD 299mg;
CALC 49mg

Broccoli With Dijon Vinaigrette

2 teaspoons olive oil
¼ cup finely chopped green onions
½ teaspoon dried tarragon
½ teaspoon dry mustard
3 garlic cloves, minced
2 tablespoons red wine vinegar
2 tablespoons water
1 tablespoon Dijon mustard
⅛ teaspoon salt
¼ teaspoon pepper
2¼ pounds fresh broccoli
Tarragon sprigs (optional)

1. Heat oil in a small saucepan over medium
heat. Add green onions and next 3 ingredients;
sauté 3 minutes. Remove from heat; add vinegar
and next 4 ingredients, stirring with a whisk until
blended. Set aside, and keep warm.

2. Remove and discard broccoli leaves and tough
ends of stalks; cut stalks into spears. Steam broccoli spears, covered, 6 minutes or until crisp-
tender. Place broccoli on a serving plate; serve
with vinaigrette. Garnish with tarragon sprigs, if
desired. Yield: 8 servings.

POINTS: 0; **Exchanges:** 1½ Veg, 1 Fat
Per serving: CAL 52 (29% from fat); PRO 4g; FAT 1.7g (sat 0.2g);
CARB 7.6g ; FIB 4.1g; CHOL 0mg; IRON 1.2mg; SOD 126mg;
CALC 67mg

Green Beans With Lemon and Browned Garlic

1 pound fresh green beans, trimmed
2½ teaspoons olive oil
3 garlic cloves, minced
3 tablespoons fresh lemon juice
⅛ teaspoon salt
⅛ teaspoon pepper

1. Bring ¾ cup water to a boil in a large nonstick
skillet; add beans, and cook 3 minutes, stirring
occasionally. Drain; set aside.

2. Heat oil in skillet over medium-high heat. Add
garlic; sauté 1 minute. Add beans; sauté 1 minute. Add lemon juice, salt, and pepper; sauté 1
minute. Yield: 4 servings (serving size: 1 cup).

POINTS: 1; **Exchanges:** 2 Veg, ½ Fat
Per serving: CAL 66 (40% from fat); PRO 2.3g; FAT 2.9g (sat 0.4g);
CARB 9.9g; FIB 2.4g; CHOL 0mg; IRON 1.2mg; SOD 78mg; CALC
47mg

**Broccoli With Dijon
Vinaigrette features the
distinctive minty flavor
of tarragon.**

Salad of Bitter Greens

Make the salad and the dressing up to four hours before serving, and chill them in separate containers.

6   cups mixed bitter greens (such as arugula, curly endive, radicchio, and watercress)
⅓   cup (1⅓ ounces) crumbled feta cheese
¼   cup chopped fresh basil
3   plum tomatoes, quartered
3   tablespoons low-salt chicken broth
2   tablespoons balsamic vinegar
1½ teaspoons olive oil
¼   teaspoon sugar
¼   teaspoon salt
¼   teaspoon freshly ground pepper
1   garlic clove, minced

1. Combine first 4 ingredients in a large bowl; toss gently.

2. Combine broth and next 6 ingredients in a bowl; stir well. Pour over salad; toss gently. Yield: 6 servings (serving size: 2 cups).

POINTS: 1; **Exchanges:** 1 Veg, ½ Fat
Per serving: CAL 57 (46% from fat); PRO 3.2g; FAT 2.9g (sat 1.1g); CARB 5.7g; FIB 2.5g; CHOL 5mg; IRON 1.6mg; SOD 182mg; CALC 78mg

Ginger-Lime Carrots

Use a food processor fitted with a slicing disc to quickly slice the carrots.

6½ cups sliced carrot (about 3 pounds)
3   tablespoons butter or margarine
3   tablespoons honey
2   tablespoons fresh lime juice
1   tablespoon grated lime rind
1   tablespoon peeled grated fresh ginger
Lime slices (optional)

1. Steam sliced carrot, covered, 10 minutes or until crisp-tender; drain.

2. Combine butter and next 4 ingredients in a large saucepan; cook over medium heat until butter melts and mixture begins to boil. Add carrots, and cook 4 minutes or until carrots are glazed, stirring constantly. Spoon into a bowl; garnish with lime slices, if desired. Yield: 6 servings (serving size: 1 cup).

POINTS: 3; **Exchanges:** 4½ Veg, ½ Starch, ½ Fat
Per serving: CAL 183 (30% from fat); PRO 2.5g; FAT 6.2g (sat 3.7g); CARB 32.4g; FIB 7.3g; CHOL 16mg; IRON 1.2mg; SOD 139mg; CALC 64mg

Corn Bread Salad

1   (8-ounce) package corn muffin mix
⅓   cup skim milk
1   large egg, lightly beaten
Cooking spray
6   cups torn romaine lettuce
1   cup seeded chopped tomato
1   cup chopped green bell pepper
¾   cup chopped red onion
3   sweet hickory-smoked bacon slices, cooked and chopped
⅔   cup fat-free ranch dressing

1. Preheat oven to 400°.

2. Combine muffin mix, milk, and egg; stir until blended. Pour batter into an 8-inch square baking pan coated with cooking spray. Bake at 400° for 15 minutes or until golden. Let cool 10 minutes. Remove corn bread from pan; cut corn bread loaf in half. Reserve half of corn bread for another use. Cut remaining half into cubes. Place corn bread cubes on a baking sheet; bake at 400° for 10 minutes or until crisp and lightly browned.

3. Combine corn bread cubes, lettuce, and next 4 ingredients; toss well. Pour dressing over salad; toss well. Serve immediately. Yield: 6 servings (serving size: 2 cups).

POINTS: 3; **Exchanges:** 1½ Starch, 1½ Veg
Per serving: CAL 152 (15% from fat); PRO 4.1g; FAT 2.6g (sat 0.5g); CARB 27.7g; FIB 1.8g; CHOL 5mg; IRON 1.6mg; SOD 501mg; CALC 37mg

Garlic Mashed Potatoes

2   pounds baking potatoes (about 4 medium), peeled and cubed
4   large garlic cloves, peeled and halved
¼   cup fat-free sour cream
2   tablespoons skim milk
1   tablespoon reduced-calorie stick margarine
½   teaspoon salt
Dash of ground white pepper

1. Place potatoes and garlic in a large saucepan; add water to cover. Bring to a boil; cover, reduce heat, and simmer 20 minutes or until tender. Drain and return potatoes and garlic to pan; beat at medium speed of a mixer 1 minute or until smooth. Add sour cream and remaining

A traditionally high-fat dish gets a healthy makeover in our Caesar Salad.

ingredients; beat until well blended. Yield: 4 servings (serving size: 1 cup).

POINTS: 3; Exchanges: 2 Starch
Per serving: CAL 163 (12% from fat); PRO 7.2g; FAT 2.1g (sat 0.1g); CARB 30.3g; FIB 4.1g; CHOL 0mg; IRON 7.4mg; SOD 357mg; CALC 82mg

Bulgur Pilaf

2   cups fat-free chicken broth
1   cup uncooked bulgur
¼   cup sliced green onions
2   tablespoons raisins
½   teaspoon salt
2   tablespoons sliced almonds, toasted

1. Bring broth to a boil in a medium saucepan. Add bulgur; cover, reduce heat, and simmer 15 minutes. Stir in green onions, raisins, and salt; cover and cook an additional 5 minutes or until bulgur is tender and liquid is absorbed. Remove from heat; stir in almonds. Yield: 4 servings (serving size: ¾ cup).

POINTS: 2; Exchanges: 2½ Starch
Per serving: CAL 200 (11% from fat); PRO 6.5g; FAT 2.5g (sat 0.3g); CARB 39.8g; FIB 8.6g; CHOL 0mg; IRON 1.2mg; SOD 304mg; CALC 31mg

Caesar Salad

¼   cup grated Parmesan cheese
¼   cup fat-free mayonnaise
¼   cup water
2   tablespoons fresh lemon juice
½   teaspoon anchovy paste
½   teaspoon Worcestershire sauce
¼   teaspoon freshly ground pepper
⅛   teaspoon dry mustard
2   garlic cloves, minced
4   (1-ounce) slices French bread, cut into ¾-inch cubes
8   cups torn romaine lettuce

1. Preheat oven to 300°.

2. Combine first 9 ingredients in a small bowl; stir well with a whisk.

3. Place bread cubes on a baking sheet, and bake at 300° for 15 minutes or until toasted. Combine croutons and lettuce in a large bowl. Add dressing, and toss to coat. Yield: 4 servings (serving size: 2 cups).

POINTS: 3; Exchanges: 2 Veg, 1 Starch, ½ Fat
Per serving: CAL 142 (15% from fat); PRO 6.8g; FAT 2.4g (sat 1.2g); CARB 22.9g; FIB 2.6g; CHOL 5mg; IRON 2mg; SOD 549mg; CALC 126mg

EDITOR'S CHOICE

Pecan Wild Rice

This test-kitchen favorite is the perfect partner for roast pork or poultry.

5½ cups chicken broth
1 cup uncooked wild rice
½ cup thinly sliced green onions
½ cup pecan halves, toasted
1 cup golden raisins
⅓ cup orange juice
¼ cup chopped fresh parsley
2 tablespoons olive oil
1 tablespoon grated orange rind
¾ teaspoon salt
¼ teaspoon freshly ground pepper

1. Combine broth and rice in a medium saucepan; bring to a boil. Reduce heat; simmer, uncovered, 45 minutes, and drain. Combine rice, green onions, and remaining ingredients in a bowl; toss gently. Yield: 6 servings (serving size: ¾ cup).

POINTS: 7; **Exchanges:** 3 Starch, 2 Fat
Per serving: CAL 321 (34% from fat); PRO 10g; FAT 12.2g (sat 1.5g); CARB 46.8g; FIB 3.4g; CHOL 0mg; IRON 2mg; SOD 948mg; CALC 44mg

Fresh Tomato-Squash Salad

3½ cups diagonally sliced small yellow squash (about 1 pound)
¾ pound small tomatoes, cut into ½-inch-thick wedges
½ cup slivered red onion
¼ cup small fresh basil leaves
¼ cup white wine vinegar
1½ teaspoons olive oil
⅛ teaspoon salt
Dash of pepper
1 garlic clove, minced

1. Steam squash slices, covered, 1 minute. Drain; plunge squash into ice water, and drain well. Combine squash, tomato wedges, onion, and basil in a large bowl.
2. Combine vinegar and next 4 ingredients in a small bowl; stir well. Pour dressing over vegetables; toss gently. Serve at room temperature. Yield: 6 servings (serving size: 1 cup).

POINTS: 1; **Exchanges:** 1 Veg, ½ Fat
Per serving: CAL 41 (33% from fat); PRO 1.4g; FAT 1.5g (sat 0.2g); CARB 6.6g; FIB 2.1g; CHOL 0mg; IRON 0.6mg; SOD 55mg; CALC 22mg

Tangy White Bean Salad

1 (15.8-ounce) can Great Northern beans, drained
1 cup seeded chopped tomato
½ cup chopped fresh parsley
½ cup chopped celery
¼ cup white wine vinegar
1½ tablespoons Dijon mustard
⅛ teaspoon white pepper

1. Combine first 4 ingredients in a medium bowl, and toss gently.
2. Combine vinegar, mustard, and pepper in a small bowl; stir well. Pour dressing over bean mixture, tossing gently. Yield: 4 servings (serving size: ¾ cup).

POINTS: 0; **Exchanges:** 1 Starch
Per serving: CAL 78 (9% from fat); PRO 3.8g; FAT 0.8g (sat 0g); CARB 13.3g; FIB 7.5g; CHOL 0mg; IRON 1.5mg; SOD 182mg; CALC 22mg

Fresh Tomato-Squash Salad makes a delicious virtue of two of summer's bumper crops.

Stewed Tomatoes and Okra

Roasted Potatoes and Artichokes With Feta

2   pounds small red potatoes, quartered
2   (14-ounce) cans quartered artichoke hearts, drained
2   tablespoons chopped fresh or 2 teaspoons dried thyme
1   tablespoon olive oil
½   teaspoon salt
¼   teaspoon pepper
Cooking spray
½   cup (2 ounces) crumbled feta cheese

1. Preheat oven to 425°.

2. Combine first 6 ingredients in a large bowl; toss well. Spoon into a 13- x 9-inch baking pan coated with cooking spray. Bake at 425° for 40 minutes or until potatoes are tender, stirring every 15 minutes. Combine potato mixture and feta cheese in a bowl; toss well. Yield: 8 servings (serving size: 1 cup).

POINTS: 3; **Exchanges:** 1½ Starch, 1½ Veg
Per serving: CAL 156 (21% from fat); PRO 6.2g; FAT 3.7g (sat 1.4g); CARB 27g; FIB 2.9g; CHOL 6mg; IRON 2.1mg; SOD 280mg; CALC 71mg

Stewed Tomatoes and Okra

3   cups frozen cut okra
1   teaspoon vegetable oil
½   cup chopped green bell pepper
¼   cup chopped onion
¼   teaspoon salt
¼   teaspoon pepper
1   (14½-ounce) can no-salt-added whole tomatoes, drained and chopped
Coarsely ground pepper (optional)

1. Combine 4 cups water and okra in a medium saucepan; bring to a boil. Reduce heat, and simmer, uncovered, 3 minutes. Drain; set aside.

2. Heat oil in saucepan over medium heat. Add bell pepper and onion; sauté 3 minutes or until tender. Add okra, salt, pepper, and tomatoes; cook until thoroughly heated. Sprinkle with coarsely ground pepper, if desired. Yield: 3 servings (serving size: 1 cup).

POINTS: 1; **Exchanges:** 3 Veg
Per serving: CAL 78 (21% from fat); PRO 3g; FAT 1.8g (sat 0.3g); CARB 14.2g; FIB 2.2g; CHOL 0mg; IRON 1.5mg; SOD 217mg; CALC 114mg

Fruited Acorn Squash

2   (1¼-pound) acorn squash
Cooking spray
¾   cup peeled chopped navel orange
3   tablespoons brown sugar
½   teaspoon ground cinnamon
1   (8-ounce) can crushed pineapple in juice, drained

1. Preheat oven to 350°.

2. Cut each squash in half lengthwise, and discard seeds and membranes. Trim bottom of each squash half to allow squash to sit flat, if necessary. Place squash halves, cut side down, in a jelly-roll pan coated with cooking spray. Bake at 350° for 35 minutes.

3. Combine chopped orange and next 3 ingredients in a bowl; stir well. Spoon evenly into squash halves. Bake at 350° an additional 15 minutes or until squash is tender. Yield: 4 servings.

Note: To microwave whole squash, pierce with a fork, and arrange on paper towels. Microwave at HIGH 9 to 10 minutes or until squash is tender. Cut in half, and remove seeds. Stuff and bake squash as directed.

POINTS: 2; **Exchanges:** ½ Fruit; 2 Starch
Per serving: CAL 161 (2% from fat); PRO 2.4g; FAT 0.3g (sat 0g); CARB 41.7g; FIB 4.8g; CHOL 0mg; IRON 1.8mg; SOD 10mg; CALC 106mg

Brussels Sprouts With Shallots

1   (16-ounce) package frozen Brussels sprouts
2   teaspoons reduced-calorie stick margarine
4   shallots, cut in half lengthwise and thinly sliced crosswise
½   cup orange juice
¼   cup water
2   tablespoons sugar
½   teaspoon chicken-flavored bouillon granules
⅛   teaspoon pepper

1. Cook Brussels sprouts according to package directions, omitting salt. Drain; set aside.

2. Melt margarine in a large nonstick skillet over medium-high heat. Add shallots; sauté 2 minutes or until tender. Add orange juice and next 4 ingredients; bring to a boil, stirring occasionally. Reduce heat, and simmer, uncovered, 3 minutes. Add Brussels sprouts, and cook 2 minutes or until thoroughly heated, stirring occasionally. Serve with a slotted spoon. Yield: 7 servings (serving size: ½ cup).

POINTS: 1; Exchanges: ½ Starch, 1 Veg
Per serving: CAL 64 (14% from fat); PRO 2.6g; FAT 1g (sat 0.1g); CARB 13.2g; FIB 2.9g; CHOL 0mg; IRON 1.1mg; SOD 87mg; CALC 33mg

Stovetop Baked Beans

You can enjoy the smoky flavor of slow-baked beans in just a few minutes with this quick and easy recipe.

1 tablespoon butter or stick margarine
1¼ cups chopped onion
¾ cup chopped green bell pepper
2 garlic cloves, minced
1 cup ketchup
¼ cup firmly packed brown sugar
¼ cup maple syrup
2 tablespoons Worcestershire sauce
2 teaspoons barbecue smoked seasoning (such as Hickory Liquid Smoke)
2 teaspoons prepared mustard
1 (16-ounce) can red beans, drained
1 (15.8-ounce) can Great Northern beans, drained

1. Melt butter in a medium saucepan over medium-high heat. Add onion, bell pepper, and garlic; sauté 4 minutes. Stir in ketchup and remaining ingredients; bring mixture to a boil. Reduce heat, and simmer, uncovered, 15 minutes, stirring occasionally. Yield: 8 servings (serving size: ½ cup).

POINTS: 3; Exchanges: 2 Starch
Per serving: CAL 180 (10% from fat); PRO 6g; FAT 1.9g (sat 0.4g); CARB 34.6g; FIB 3.8g; CHOL 0mg; IRON 2mg; SOD 331mg; CALC 53mg

Marinated Vegetable Salad

½ cup fat-free Italian dressing
¼ cup sliced green onions
¼ cup balsamic vinegar
1 (14-ounce) can quartered artichoke hearts, drained
1 (8-ounce) package presliced fresh mushrooms
1 medium zucchini, thinly sliced
4 cups torn curly leaf lettuce
1 cup cherry tomatoes, halved
¾ cup (½-inch) cubed part-skim mozzarella cheese (about 4 ounces)
¼ cup sliced ripe olives
2 tablespoons grated fresh Parmesan cheese

1. Combine first 6 ingredients in a large bowl; stir well. Cover and marinate in refrigerator up to 4 hours, stirring occasionally.

2. Drain vegetables; discard marinade. Combine marinated vegetables, lettuce, and next 3 ingredients in a large bowl; toss gently to coat. Sprinkle with Parmesan cheese. Yield: 6 servings (serving size: 2 cups).

POINTS: 3; Exchanges: 2 Veg, ½ Starch, 1 Fat
Per serving: CAL 128 (32% from fat); PRO 9.2g; FAT 4.6g (sat 0.5g); CARB 15.3g; FIB 1.6g; CHOL 12mg; IRON 2.2mg; SOD 449mg; CALC 201mg

Hash Brown Casserole

1 cup thinly sliced green onions
1 cup (4 ounces) shredded reduced-fat sharp cheddar cheese
2 tablespoons stick margarine, melted
¼ teaspoon pepper
1 (32-ounce) package frozen Southern-style hash brown potatoes, thawed
1 (16-ounce) carton fat-free sour cream
1 (10¾-ounce) can condensed reduced-fat reduced-salt cream of mushroom soup, undiluted
Cooking spray
½ teaspoon paprika

1. Preheat oven to 350°.

2. Combine first 7 ingredients in a large bowl, and stir well. Spoon mixture into a 13- x 9-inch baking dish coated with cooking spray. Sprinkle paprika evenly over casserole. Bake at 350° for 1 hour or until bubbly. Yield: 9 servings (serving size: 1 cup).

POINTS: 3; Exchanges: 1 Starch, 1 Fat, ½ Veg
Per serving: CAL 146 (27% from fat); PRO 6.7g; FAT 4.3g (sat 1.5g); CARB 17.8g; FIB 0.7g; CHOL 8mg; IRON 0.7mg; SOD 224mg; CALC 105mg

Hash Brown Casserole

Blue-Ribbon Breads

T*here are two reasons we love to make bread: First, it makes your house smell like a home, and second, nothing tastes better than the fresh-baked goodness of homemade bread. Whether in the form of yeast biscuits, fruit-flecked muffins, or a tender, sweet loaf, home-baked bread is a true crowd pleaser. And as you'll find with the recipes on the following pages, baking bread doesn't have to be difficult. We've discovered a few convenience products that cut down on preparation time. For example, Easy Focaccia (page 64) takes advantage of frozen bread dough, and Apple Butter-Banana Muffins (page 65) uses a muffin mix. But don't tell; it will still smell like you slaved for hours.*

Dill Pickle Rye Bread tastes like a deli sandwich—minus the meat.

Buttermilk Pancakes

Dill Pickle Rye Bread

The acid from the pickles and pickle juice in the dough keeps these loaves from rising as high as a typical yeast bread. Even so, the texture is moist and these hearty loaves are full of flavor.

3   cups all-purpose flour
3   cups rye flour
2   packages dry yeast
1   cup finely chopped dill pickles
1   cup water
½   cup dill pickle juice
½   cup low-fat buttermilk
¼   cup vegetable oil
2   tablespoons sugar
2   teaspoons dill seeds
2   teaspoons caraway seeds
1   teaspoon salt
Cooking spray

1. Combine flours in a large bowl, and stir well. Remove 2 cups flour mixture, and place in a large bowl of a heavy-duty stand mixer. Add yeast; stir well, and set aside.

2. Combine chopped dill pickles and next 8 ingredients in a medium saucepan. Place over medium-high heat, and cook until mixture reaches 120° to 130°, stirring occasionally. Gradually add pickle mixture to flour-yeast mixture, beating at low speed of mixer until blended. Beat an additional 2 minutes at medium speed. Gradually stir in enough of remaining flour mixture to form a soft dough.

3. Turn dough out onto a lightly floured surface, and knead 8 minutes or until smooth and elastic. Place in a large bowl coated with cooking spray, turning to coat top. Cover and let rise in a warm place (85°), free from drafts, 40 minutes or until doubled in bulk.

4. Punch dough down; turn out onto a lightly floured surface, and knead lightly 4 or 5 times. Divide dough in half. Roll each portion into a 14- x 7-inch rectangle. Roll up each rectangle, starting with a short edge, pressing firmly to eliminate air pockets; pinch seams and ends to seal. Place each roll, seam side down, in an 8- x 4-inch loaf pan coated with cooking spray.

5. Cover and let rise 40 minutes or until doubled in bulk.

6. Preheat oven to 350°.

7. Bake at 350° for 40 minutes or until loaves sound hollow when tapped. Remove bread from pans immediately; let cool on wire racks. Yield: 2 loaves, 12 servings per loaf (serving size: 1 slice).

POINTS: 2; **Exchanges:** 1½ Starch
Per serving: CAL 132 (19% from fat); PRO 3.3g; FAT 2.8g (sat 0.5g); CARB 23.8g; FIB 2.6g; CHOL 0mg; IRON 1.3mg; SOD 272mg; CALC 19mg

Buttermilk Pancakes

To freeze, place wax paper between pancakes and store in a zip-top plastic bag or wrap tightly in foil.

1   cup all-purpose flour
2   tablespoons sugar
1   teaspoon baking powder
½   teaspoon baking soda
¼   teaspoon salt
1   cup low-fat buttermilk
1   tablespoon vegetable oil
1   large egg, lightly beaten
Cooking spray

1. Combine first 5 ingredients in a large bowl; stir well, and make a well in center of mixture. Combine buttermilk, oil, and egg; stir well. Add to flour mixture, stirring just until moist.

2. Pour ¼ cup batter for each pancake onto a hot nonstick griddle or nonstick skillet. Turn pancakes when tops are covered with bubbles and edges look cooked. Yield: 3 servings (serving size: 3 [4-inch] pancakes).

POINTS: 6; **Exchanges:** 3 Starch, 1 Fat
Per serving: CAL 291 (25% from fat); PRO 9.5g; FAT 8g (sat 1.4g); CARB 44.6g; FIB 1.1g; CHOL 74mg; IRON 2.2mg; SOD 598mg; CALC 184mg

Huckleberry Coffee Cake

¼   cup stick margarine, softened
4   ounces block-style fat-free cream cheese (about ½ cup)
1   cup sugar
1   large egg
1   cup all-purpose flour
1   teaspoon baking powder
¼   teaspoon salt
1   teaspoon vanilla extract

2 cups fresh or frozen huckleberries or blueberries, unthawed
Cooking spray
2 tablespoons sugar
1 teaspoon ground cinnamon

1. Preheat oven to 350°.

2. Beat margarine and cream cheese at medium speed of a mixer just until creamy (do not overbeat); gradually add 1 cup sugar, beating just until blended. Add egg; beat just until blended.

3. Combine flour, baking powder, and salt; stir into margarine mixture. Stir in vanilla; fold in berries. Pour batter into a 9-inch round cake pan coated with cooking spray. Combine 2 tablespoons sugar and cinnamon; sprinkle over batter.

4. Bake at 350° for 1 hour; let cool on a wire rack.

Yield: 10 servings (serving size: 1 wedge).

POINTS: 4; **Exchanges:** 2½ Starch, ½ Fat
Per serving: CAL 209 (23% from fat); PRO 3.7g; FAT 5.3g (sat 1g); CARB 36.9g; FIB 1.7g; CHOL 24mg; IRON 0.8mg; SOD 188mg; CALC 70mg

Orange-Glazed Cranberry-Pumpkin Bread

Lightly drizzled with a sweet orange glaze, this moist loaf bread features tart cranberries, pumpkin, and walnuts.

3½ cups all-purpose flour
1⅔ cups sugar
2 teaspoons baking soda
2 teaspoons pumpkin pie spice
1 teaspoon baking powder
¾ teaspoon salt
⅔ cup vegetable oil
1 (16-ounce) can whole-berry cranberry sauce
1 (15-ounce) can pumpkin
4 large eggs, lightly beaten
¾ cup chopped walnuts
Cooking spray
Orange Glaze

1. Preheat oven to 350°.

2. Combine first 6 ingredients in a large bowl; stir well, and make a well in center of mixture.

3. Combine oil and next 3 ingredients in a bowl, and stir well. Add to flour mixture, stirring just until blended. Stir in walnuts. Pour batter into 2 (9- x 5-inch) loaf pans coated with cooking spray.

4. Bake at 350° for 1 hour or until a wooden pick inserted in center comes out clean. Let cool in pans 10 minutes on wire racks; remove from pans, and let cool completely on wire racks. Drizzle Orange Glaze evenly over loaves. Yield: 2 loaves, 12 servings per loaf (serving size: 1 slice).

POINTS: 6; **Exchanges:** 3 Starch, 1 Fat
Per serving: CAL 267 (31% from fat); PRO 4g; FAT 9.3g (sat 1.5g); CARB 43.2g; FIB 1.6g; CHOL 30mg; IRON 1.4mg; SOD 215mg; CALC 27mg

Orange Glaze:

1 cup sifted powdered sugar
¼ cup thawed orange juice concentrate, undiluted
⅛ teaspoon ground allspice

1. Combine all ingredients in a small bowl, stirring until smooth. Yield: ½ cup.

Orange Gingerbread Muffins

2 cups low-fat biscuit and baking mix (such as Bisquick)
¼ cup cinnamon-sugar, divided
½ teaspoon ground ginger
⅔ cup skim milk
¼ cup molasses
1 tablespoon grated orange rind
1 large egg, lightly beaten
Butter-flavored cooking spray

1. Preheat oven to 400°.

2. Combine biscuit and baking mix, 3½ tablespoons cinnamon-sugar, and ginger in a large bowl; stir well, and make a well in center of mixture. Combine milk and next 3 ingredients in a bowl; stir well. Add to dry ingredients, stirring just until moist.

3. Divide batter evenly among muffin cups coated with cooking spray; sprinkle remaining 1½ teaspoons cinnamon-sugar over batter. Bake at 400° for 12 minutes. Remove from pans immediately. Yield: 1 dozen (serving size: 1 muffin).

POINTS: 3; **Exchanges:** 1½ Starch
Per serving: CAL 122 (14% from fat); PRO 2.5g; FAT 2g (sat 0.4g); CARB 24g; FIB 0.3g; CHOL 19mg; IRON 0.8mg; SOD 247mg; CALC 83mg

Picante Corn Bread Muffins

1½ cups yellow cornmeal
1   teaspoon baking soda
1   teaspoon sugar
½   teaspoon salt
¼   cup picante sauce
3   tablespoons vegetable oil
1   (8-ounce) carton plain fat-free yogurt
2   large egg whites
Cooking spray

1. Preheat oven to 425°.

2. Combine first 4 ingredients in a large bowl; stir well. Make a well in center of mixture. Combine picante sauce and next 3 ingredients; stir well. Add to cornmeal mixture, stirring just until moist.

3. Divide batter evenly among muffin cups coated with cooking spray. Bake at 425° for 18 minutes or until golden. Remove from pans immediately. Yield: 1 dozen (serving size: 1 muffin).

POINTS: 2; **Exchanges:** 1 Starch, ½ Fat
Per serving: CAL 102 (35% from fat); PRO 2.9g; FAT 4g (sat 0.6g); CARB 13.9g; FIB 1.7g; CHOL 0mg; IRON 0.6mg; SOD 287mg; CALC 40mg

Refrigerator Yeast Rolls

1   package dry yeast
¼   cup warm water (105° to 115°)
¼   cup plus 2 tablespoons sugar, divided
1¾   cups skim milk
¼   cup vegetable oil
1½   teaspoons salt
6   cups plus 1 tablespoon bread flour, divided
Butter-flavored cooking spray

1. Combine yeast, warm water, and 1 teaspoon sugar in a small bowl; let stand 5 minutes. Combine remaining sugar, milk, oil, and salt in a small saucepan; cook over medium heat until sugar dissolves, stirring occasionally. Let cool to 115°. Add yeast mixture to warm milk mixture, stirring well with a whisk.

2. Place 6 cups flour in a large bowl. Gradually add milk mixture to flour, stirring to form a stiff dough. Place dough in a large bowl coated with cooking spray, turning to coat top. Let stand at room temperature 10 minutes. Cover and refrigerate at least 8 hours (dough may remain in refrigerator up to 5 days.)

3. Sprinkle remaining 1 tablespoon flour over work surface. Punch dough down; turn out onto floured surface, and knead 2 or 3 times. Divide dough into 3 equal portions. Working with 1 portion at a time (cover remaining portions to keep dough from drying out), shape each portion into 12 balls. Place balls in a 9-inch round cake pan coated with cooking spray. Repeat procedure with remaining portions of dough. Cover and let rise in a warm place (85°), free from drafts, 45 minutes or until doubled in bulk.

4. Preheat oven to 400°.

5. Bake at 400° for 10 minutes or until golden. Coat rolls lightly with cooking spray. Yield: 3 dozen (serving size: 1 roll).

POINTS: 2; **Exchanges:** 1½ Starch
Per serving: CAL 111 (17% from fat); PRO 3.2g; FAT 2.1g (sat 0.4g); CARB 19.5g; FIB 0.6g; CHOL 0mg; IRON 1.1mg; SOD 104mg; CALC 18mg

EDITOR'S CHOICE

Refrigerator Yeast Rolls will remind you of the ones your grandma made.

Fruit-filled Pear-and-Poppy Seed Loaf makes a satisfying breakfast or snack.

Pear-and-Poppy Seed Loaf

2¼ cups all-purpose flour
3   tablespoons poppy seeds
1½ teaspoons baking powder
1   teaspoon baking soda
½   teaspoon salt
⅛   teaspoon ground cardamom
1   cup peeled chopped ripe pear
1   cup low-fat buttermilk
⅔   cup sugar
¼   cup honey
2   tablespoons stick margarine, melted
1   teaspoon vanilla extract
1   large egg
Cooking spray

1. Preheat oven to 350°.

2. Combine first 6 ingredients in a large bowl; stir well. Stir in pear; make a well in center of mixture. Combine buttermilk and next 5 ingredients in a bowl; stir well with a whisk. Add to flour mixture, stirring just until moist. Spoon batter into an 8- x 4-inch loaf pan coated with cooking spray.

3. Bake at 350° for 1 hour and 5 minutes or until a wooden pick inserted in center comes out clean. Let cool in pan 10 minutes on a wire rack, and remove from pan. Let cool completely on wire rack. Yield: 14 servings.

POINTS: 4; **Exchanges:** 2 Starch
Per serving: CAL 173 (17% from fat); PRO 3.6g; FAT 3.2g (sat 0.6g); CARB 33.2g; FIB 1g; CHOL 16mg; IRON 1.3mg; SOD 217mg; CALC 84mg

Buttermilk-Apricot Scones

Delicate scones are best when served hot. The wedges that taste heavenly just minutes out of the oven often seem dry and less flavorful after they cool.

2   cups all-purpose flour
¼   cup sugar
1½ teaspoons baking powder
½   teaspoon baking soda
¼   teaspoon salt
¼   cup chilled stick margarine, cut into small pieces
⅓   cup chopped dried apricots
¼   cup low-fat buttermilk
¼   cup apricot nectar
1   large egg, lightly beaten
Cooking spray
1   large egg white, lightly beaten
1   tablespoon sugar

1. Preheat oven to 400°.

2. Combine first 5 ingredients in a large bowl; cut in margarine with a pastry blender or 2 knives until mixture resembles coarse meal. Add apricots; toss well. Combine buttermilk, nectar, and egg in a bowl; stir well. Add to flour mixture, stirring just until moist (dough will be sticky).

3. Turn dough out onto a lightly floured surface; with floured hands, knead 4 or 5 times. Pat dough into a 9-inch circle on a baking sheet coated with cooking spray. Cut dough into 12 wedges, cutting to, but not through, bottom of dough. Brush with egg white, and sprinkle with 1 tablespoon sugar. Bake at 400° for 15 minutes or until golden. Serve hot. Yield: 12 servings.

POINTS: 3; **Exchanges:** 1½ Starch, ½ Fat
Per serving: CAL 152 (27% from fat); PRO 3.3g; FAT 4.5g (sat 0.9g); CARB 24.6g; FIB 0.9g; CHOL 18mg; IRON 1.3mg; SOD 220mg; CALC 49mg

Carrot-Raisin Quick Bread

1¾ cups all-purpose flour
1   teaspoon baking soda
¾   teaspoon ground cinnamon
¼   teaspoon salt
¼   teaspoon baking powder
¼   teaspoon ground nutmeg
1   cup coarsely shredded carrot
⅔   cup firmly packed brown sugar
½   cup golden raisins
½   cup skim milk
3   tablespoons butter or stick margarine, melted
1   large egg, lightly beaten
Cooking spray

1. Preheat oven to 350°.

2. Combine first 6 ingredients in a large bowl. Combine carrot and next 5 ingredients; stir well. Add to flour mixture, stirring just until moist.

3. Pour batter into an 8- x 4-inch loaf pan coated with cooking spray. Bake at 350° for 1 hour and 5 minutes or until a wooden pick inserted in center comes out clean. Let cool in pan 10 minutes on a wire rack; remove from pan. Let cool completely on a wire rack. Yield: 12 servings.

POINTS: 4; **Exchanges:** 2 Starch
Per serving: CAL 174 (19% from fat); PRO 3.1g; FAT 3.6g (sat 0.8g); CARB 32.9g; FIB 1.2g; CHOL 19mg; IRON 1.4mg; SOD 215mg; CALC 42mg

Black Forest Bread

1¾ cups all-purpose flour
½ cup unsweetened cocoa
1 teaspoon baking soda
½ teaspoon salt
½ cup dried cherries or dried sweetened cranberries (such as Craisins)
1 tablespoon hot water
2 teaspoons instant coffee granules
¾ cup low-fat buttermilk
⅔ cup sugar
⅓ cup honey
2 tablespoons vegetable oil
2 teaspoons vanilla extract
1 large egg
Cooking spray

1. Preheat oven to 350°.

2. Combine first 4 ingredients in a bowl; stir well. Stir in cherries; make a well in center of mixture. Combine hot water and coffee granules in a bowl; stir well. Add buttermilk and next 5 ingredients, stirring well with a whisk. Add to flour mixture, stirring just until moist. Spoon batter into an 8- x 4-inch loaf pan coated with cooking spray.

3. Bake at 350° for 50 minutes or until a wooden pick inserted in center comes out clean. Let cool in pan 10 minutes on a wire rack; remove from pan. Let cool on wire rack. Yield: 14 servings.

POINTS: 4; **Exchanges:** 2½ Starch
Per serving: CAL 178 (15% from fat); PRO 3.7g; FAT 3g (sat 0.8g); CARB 34.5g; FIB 0.7g; CHOL 16mg; IRON 1.5mg; SOD 195mg; CALC 28mg

Angel Biscuits

1 package dry yeast
½ cup warm water (105° to 115°)
5 cups all-purpose flour
¼ cup sugar
1 teaspoon baking powder
1 teaspoon baking soda
1 teaspoon salt
½ cup vegetable shortening
2 cups low-fat buttermilk
Cooking spray
1 tablespoon butter or stick margarine, melted

1. Dissolve yeast in warm water in a small bowl; let stand 5 minutes.

2. Combine flour and next 4 ingredients in a large bowl; cut in shortening with a pastry blender or 2 knives until mixture resembles coarse meal. Add yeast mixture and buttermilk; stir just until moist. Cover and chill 1 hour.

3. Preheat oven to 450°.

4. Turn dough out onto a heavily floured surface; knead lightly 5 times. Roll dough to a ½-inch thickness; cut with a 3-inch biscuit cutter. Place biscuits on a baking sheet coated with cooking spray. Brush melted butter over biscuit tops. Bake

Coffee and cocoa combine to impart a rich, chocolaty flavor to Black Forest Bread.

at 450° for 13 minutes or until golden. Yield: 2 dozen (serving size: 1 biscuit).

POINTS: 3; **Exchanges:** 1½ Starch, ½ Fat
Per serving: CAL 150 (28% from fat); PRO 3.6g; FAT 4.6g (sat 1.2g); CARB 23.1g; FIB 0.8g; CHOL 0mg; IRON 1.3mg; SOD 183mg; CALC 41mg

Blueberry-Yogurt Muffins

2   cups all-purpose flour
⅓   cup sugar
1   teaspoon baking powder
1   teaspoon baking soda
¼   teaspoon salt
¼   cup orange juice
2   tablespoons vegetable oil
1   teaspoon vanilla extract
1   (8-ounce) carton vanilla low-fat yogurt
1   large egg, lightly beaten
1   cup fresh or frozen blueberries, thawed
Cooking spray
1   tablespoon sugar

1. Preheat oven to 400°.

2. Combine first 5 ingredients in a large bowl; stir well, and make a well in center of mixture. Combine orange juice and next 4 ingredients in a bowl; stir well. Add to flour mixture, stirring just until moist. Gently fold in blueberries.

3. Divide batter evenly among 12 muffin cups coated with cooking spray; sprinkle 1 tablespoon sugar evenly over batter. Bake at 400° for 18 minutes or until golden. Remove from pans immediately; let cool on a wire rack. Yield: 1 dozen (serving size: 1 muffin).

POINTS: 3; **Exchanges:** 2 Starch
Per serving: CAL 153 (19% from fat); PRO 3.7g; FAT 3.3g (sat 0.7g); CARB 27.2g; FIB 0.9g; CHOL 19mg; IRON 1.1mg; SOD 172mg; CALC 62mg

Macadamia Nut-Banana Bread

Macadamia nuts add a tropical flair to this banana bread, but you can substitute an equal amount of any type nut.

2¼   cups all-purpose flour
¾   cup firmly packed brown sugar
¼   cup sugar
3½   teaspoons baking powder
1½   teaspoons ground cinnamon
½   teaspoon salt

1¼   cups mashed ripe banana
⅓   cup skim milk
3   tablespoons vegetable oil
1   teaspoon white vinegar
1   large egg
½   cup macadamia nuts, coarsely chopped
Cooking spray

1. Preheat oven to 350°.

2. Combine first 6 ingredients in a large bowl; stir well, and make a well in center of mixture. Combine banana and next 4 ingredients; stir with a whisk until blended. Add to flour mixture, stirring just until moist. Stir in macadamia nuts.

3. Spoon batter into a 9- x 5-inch loaf pan coated with cooking spray. Bake at 350° for 1 hour or until a wooden pick inserted in center comes out clean. Let cool in pan 10 minutes on a wire rack. Remove from pan, and let cool completely on wire rack. Yield: 12 servings.

POINTS: 5; **Exchanges:** 2½ Starch, 1 Fat
Per serving: CAL 237 (32% from fat); PRO 3.9g; FAT 8.3g (sat 1.5g); CARB 38.1g; FIB 1.6g; CHOL 19mg; IRON 1.8mg; SOD 254mg; CALC 110mg

Basil Batter Rolls

These pesto-flavored batter rolls couldn't be any easier—no kneading.

2   packages dry yeast
1½   cups warm water (105° to 115°)
4   cups unbleached or all-purpose flour, divided
⅓   cup vegetable shortening
¼   cup sugar
1½   teaspoons salt
1   large egg
2   tablespoons prepared pesto (such as Pesto Sanremo)
2   garlic cloves, minced
Cooking spray

1. Dissolve yeast in warm water in a large bowl; let stand 5 minutes. Add 2 cups flour and next 4 ingredients; beat at medium speed of a mixer until well blended. Stir in pesto and garlic. Gradually stir in enough remaining flour to form a soft dough (dough will be sticky).

2. Cover and let rise in a warm place (85°), free from drafts, 50 minutes or until doubled in bulk.

Blueberry-Yogurt Muffins

1. Combine yeast packet from roll mix and warm water in a large bowl. Let stand 5 minutes. Add three-fourths of flour packet from roll mix, cheese, and next 4 ingredients; beat at low speed of a mixer until blended. Stir in remaining flour from roll mix.

2. Scrape dough from sides of bowl. Cover; let rise in a warm place (85°), free from drafts, 30 minutes or until doubled in bulk. Stir dough 25 strokes.

3. Preheat oven to 350°.

4. Coat a 2-quart casserole dish with cooking spray. Spoon dough into dish. Bake at 350° for 45 minutes or until loaf is browned and sounds hollow when tapped. Yield: 14 servings.

POINTS: 4; Exchanges: 1½ Starch, 1 Fat
Per serving: CAL 160 (25% from fat); PRO 6.1g; FAT 4.4g (sat 1.1g); CARB 23.1g; FIB 0.7g; CHOL 5mg; IRON 0.7mg; SOD 246mg; CALC 101mg

Easy Focaccia

Gently press your finger into dough at 2-inch intervals to create dimples before brushing with olive oil.

2   (1-pound) loaves frozen white bread dough, thawed
Cooking spray
2   tablespoons olive oil
1   small onion, thinly sliced and separated into rings
¼   cup grated Parmesan cheese
1   teaspoon dried rosemary
½   teaspoon garlic powder

1. Preheat oven to 375°.

2. Place loaves of dough on each of 2 baking sheets coated with cooking spray; press each portion of dough into a 12- x 8-inch rectangle. Brush oil evenly over dough. Top with onion rings, and sprinkle evenly with cheese, rosemary, and garlic powder. Bake at 375° for 25 minutes or until lightly browned. Serve warm or let cool completely on wire racks. Yield: 2 loaves, 12 servings per loaf (serving size: 1 slice).

POINTS: 3; Exchanges: 1½ Starch
Per serving: CAL 128 (18% from fat); PRO 5g; FAT 2.5g (sat 0.3g); CARB 21.3g; FIB 0.1g; CHOL 1mg; IRON 1.3mg; SOD 276mg; CALC 23mg

Easy Focaccia blends the flavors of onion, rosemary, and olive oil.

3. Stir dough, and divide evenly among muffin cups coated with cooking spray. Cover and let rise 45 minutes.

4. Preheat oven to 400°.

5. Bake at 400° for 15 minutes or until golden. Yield: 2 dozen (serving size: 1 roll).

POINTS: 3; Exchanges: 1 Starch, 1 Fat
Per serving: CAL 122 (30% from fat); PRO 3.2g; FAT 4g (sat 0.9g); CARB 18.3g; FIB 0.2g; CHOL 9mg; IRON 1mg; SOD 286mg; CALC 15mg

Caraway-Swiss Casserole Bread

1   (16-ounce) box hot roll mix (such as Pillsbury)
1⅓ cups warm water (105° to 115°)
1   cup (4 ounces) shredded reduced-fat Swiss cheese
¼   cup finely chopped onion
2   tablespoons stick margarine, melted
1   tablespoon caraway seeds
1   teaspoon cracked pepper
Cooking spray

Apple Butter-Banana Muffins

1   (7.4-ounce) package banana-nut muffin
    mix (such as Betty Crocker)
⅓ cup apple butter
½ cup chopped dates
1   tablespoon skim milk
1   large egg, lightly beaten
Cooking spray

1. Preheat oven to 450°.

2. Combine first 5 ingredients in a bowl, stirring just until moist. Divide batter evenly among 8 muffin cups coated with cooking spray.

3. Bake at 450° for 10 minutes or until lightly browned. Remove from pans immediately. Yield: 8 muffins (serving size: 1 muffin).

POINTS: 4; **Exchanges:** 1½ Starch, 1 Fruit, ½ Fat
Per serving: CAL 213 (21% from fat); PRO 3.5g; FAT 5g (sat 1.3g); CARB 39.5g; FIB 1.1g; CHOL 37mg; IRON 1mg; SOD 243mg; CALC 13mg

Spoon Bread

2¼ cups skim milk, divided
⅔ cup cornmeal
2   tablespoons stick margarine, melted
⅛ teaspoon salt
¼ teaspoon pepper
1   (8-ounce) carton egg substitute
Cooking spray

1. Preheat oven to 375°.

2. Heat 2 cups milk over medium-high heat in a heavy saucepan to 180° or until tiny bubbles form around edge (do not boil). Place cornmeal in a bowl. Add remaining ¼ cup milk, margarine, salt, and pepper, stirring until well blended; add to saucepan. Bring to a boil over medium-high heat, stirring constantly with a wire whisk; cook 2 minutes or until thick, stirring constantly. Remove from heat, and set aside.

3. Beat egg substitute in a bowl at high speed of a mixer 2 minutes or until slightly thick. Add egg substitute to cornmeal mixture; stir until well blended. Pour into a 1½-quart casserole coated with cooking spray. Bake at 375° for 30 minutes or until puffed and set; serve immediately. Yield 4 servings (serving size: ¾ cup).

POINTS: 5; **Exchanges:** 1½ Starch, ½ Sk Milk, ½ Very Lean Meat, ½ Fat
Per serving: CAL 213 (27% from fat); PRO 12.3g; FAT 6.5g (sat 1.3g); CARB 25.6g; FIB 1.2g; CHOL 2.7mg; IRON 2mg; SOD 297mg; CALC 193mg

Popovers

1   cup bread flour
1   cup 1% low-fat milk
¾ cup egg substitute
1   tablespoon sugar
1   tablespoon vegetable oil
¼ teaspoon salt
Cooking spray

1. Place first 6 ingredients in a food processor; process until smooth.

2. Pour batter evenly into popover pans coated with cooking spray. Place in a cold oven. Turn oven temperature to 450°, and bake 15 minutes. Reduce oven temperature to 350°, and bake 35 minutes or until popovers are crusty and brown. Yield: 8 popovers (serving size: 1 popover).

POINTS: 2; **Exchanges:** 1 Starch, ½ Fat
Per serving: CAL 109 (21% from fat); PRO 5.3g; FAT 2.5g (sat 0.6g); CARB 15.9g; FIB 0.4g; CHOL 1mg; IRON 1mg; SOD 123mg; CALC 48mg

Peppered Pimiento Cheese Bread

¾ cup (3 ounces) preshredded reduced-fat
    Mexican cheese blend
½ cup fat-free mayonnaise
3   tablespoons chopped green onions
2   tablespoons diced pimiento
½ teaspoon pepper
2   (2½-ounce) submarine rolls

1. Preheat oven to 400°.

2. Combine first 5 ingredients in a medium bowl, and stir well.

3. Cut each roll in half lengthwise, and then in half crosswise. Spread cheese mixture evenly over cut sides of rolls. Place rolls on a baking sheet; bake at 400° for 8 minutes or until cheese melts. Yield: 8 servings.

POINTS: 2; **Exchanges:** 1 Starch, ½ Fat
Per serving: CAL 94 (25% from fat); PRO 5g; FAT 2.6g (sat 1.3g); CARB 13.2g; FIB 0.5g; CHOL 4mg; IRON 0.7mg; SOD 370mg; CALC 93mg

Award-Winning Appetizers and Snacks

YOU WON'T FEEL GUILTY SATISFYING YOUR HUNGER WITH THESE HEALTHFUL SNACKS.

Remember when snacking between meals was a no-no? You'd get so hungry that by the time mealtime rolled around, it was nearly impossible to make smart choices. Today we know snacks can be key to healthful eating, as long as they satisfy your cravings without using up all your mealtime POINTS. And many of the recipes on the following pages can be made in advance so they're ready and waiting for you. Keep a container of our creamy Hummus Spread (page 74) handy in the fridge or our Peanut Butter-Granola Gorp (page 73) in the pantry, and you won't be tempted to reach for potato chips.

Chilling in an icy bowl, Creamy Pineapple Pops (page 69) can chase the heat away on the hottest day.

Italian-Seasoned Snack Mix

Creamy Pineapple Pops

This recipe doubles easily so you can always have a cool, refreshing treat on hand.

1   (15¼-ounce) can crushed pineapple in juice, undrained
1   (8-ounce) carton pineapple low-fat yogurt
3   tablespoons honey
1   tablespoon chopped fresh mint (optional)
6   (6-ounce) paper cups or popsicle molds
6   wooden popsicle sticks

1. Combine first 3 ingredients in a small bowl. Stir in mint, if desired.

2. Spoon pineapple mixture evenly into paper cups or popsicle molds. Cover tops of cups with foil, and insert a wooden stick through foil into center of each cup. Freeze until firm. To serve, remove foil; peel cup from pop. Yield: 6 servings.

Note: For testing, we used Williams-Sonoma's durable plastic molds. Call 1-800-840-2591 to order the pop mold (which makes six) or the bar mold (which makes eight); each costs $16.

POINTS: 2; Exchanges: 1 Starch, ½ Fruit
Per serving: CAL 113 (4% from fat); PRO 1.8g; FAT 0.5g (sat 0.3g); CARB 27.1g; FIB 0.6g; CHOL 2mg; IRON 0.2mg; SOD 21mg; CALC 59mg

Italian-Seasoned Snack Mix

4   cups criss-cross of corn and rice cereal (such as Crispix)
2   cups oyster crackers
2   cups tiny fat-free pretzels
¼   cup reduced-calorie stick margarine, melted
2   large egg whites
¼   cup grated Parmesan cheese
1   tablespoon dried Italian seasoning
    Cooking spray

1. Preheat oven to 300°.

2. Combine first 3 ingredients in a large bowl. Combine margarine and egg whites in a small bowl, stirring well with a whisk. Pour margarine mixture over cereal mixture; toss gently to coat. Sprinkle cheese and Italian seasoning evenly over cereal mixture; toss gently.

3. Divide mixture between 2 jelly-roll pans coated with cooking spray, spreading evenly. Bake at 300° for 25 minutes or until crisp, stirring occasionally. Let cool completely. Store in an airtight container. Yield: 24 servings (serving size: ¼ cup).

POINTS: 1; Exchanges: ½ Starch, ½ Fat
Per serving: CAL 62 (29% from fat); PRO 1.6g; FAT 2g (sat 0.3g); CARB 9.9g; FIB 0.5g; CHOL 1mg; IRON 0.9mg; SOD 188mg; CALC 22mg

Caramel-Apple Crisps

We recommend using either a Golden Delicious or a Red Delicious apple for this simple, low-*POINT* snack.

6   (4-inch) fat-free caramel-flavored popcorn cakes
1   medium apple, cored and thinly sliced
1½ tablespoons fat-free caramel-flavored sundae syrup
1   tablespoon brown sugar
½   teaspoon ground cinnamon

1. Place popcorn cakes on a baking sheet. Top evenly with sliced apple; drizzle caramel syrup evenly over apple. Combine brown sugar and cinnamon; sprinkle evenly over each serving. Broil 3 minutes. Serve immediately. Yield: 6 servings.

POINTS: 2; Exchanges: 1½ Fruit
Per serving: CAL 84 (1% from fat); PRO 1.1; FAT 0.1g (sat 0g); CARB 20.6g; FIB 0.8g; CHOL 0mg; IRON 0.4; SOD 40mg; CALC 11mg

Turn popcorn cakes and a bit of apple into an occasion with Caramel-Apple Crisps.

Tropical S'mores

¼ cup drained canned crushed pineapple
    in juice
¼ cup peeled chopped papaya
1 teaspoon fresh lime juice
4 sheets low-fat graham crackers
½ cup miniature marshmallows
2 teaspoons flaked sweetened coconut

1. Combine first 3 ingredients in a small bowl.

2. Place graham crackers on a baking sheet; top evenly with marshmallows, pineapple mixture, and coconut. Broil 40 seconds or until lightly browned. Serve immediately. Yield: 4 servings.

POINTS: 2; **Exchanges:** 1½ Starch
Per serving: CAL 116 (7% from fat); PRO 1.3g; FAT 0.9g (sat 0.5g); CARB 26.2g; FIB 0.9g; CHOL 0mg; IRON 0.6mg; SOD 105mg; CALC 8mg

Garlic-Cheese Toasts

½ cup tub-style light cream cheese, softened
1½ tablespoons chopped fresh chives
1 tablespoon grated fat-free Parmesan cheese
1 garlic clove, minced
24 (½-inch-thick) slices French bread
    baguette, toasted

1. Combine first 4 ingredients in a small bowl, and stir until well blended. Spread 1 teaspoon cream cheese mixture over 1 side of each toasted baguette slice. Yield: 24 servings.

POINTS: 1; **Exchanges:** ½ Starch
Per serving: CAL 36 (25% from fat); PRO 1.4g; FAT 1g (sat 0.5g); CARB 5.2g; FIB 0.1g; CHOL 3mg; IRON 0.6mg; SOD 79mg; CALC 28mg

Sweet Onion Spread

⅔ cup tub-style light cream cheese, softened
⅓ cup sweet onion relish
2 tablespoons fat-free mayonnaise
¼ teaspoon pepper
32 pieces melba toast

1. Combine first 4 ingredients in a medium bowl; stir well. Spread 1½ teaspoons cream cheese mixture over 1 side of each piece melba toast. Yield: 8 servings.

POINTS: 1; **Exchanges:** 1 Starch, ½ Fat
Per serving: CAL 102 (34% from fat); PRO 3.6g; FAT 3.9g (sat 1.8g); CARB 13.6g; FIB 0g; CHOL 11mg; IRON 0.6mg; SOD 338mg; CALC 26mg

Pineapple Cheese Ball

1 (8-ounce) can crushed pineapple in juice,
    well drained
¾ cup (3 ounces) shredded fat-free sharp
    cheddar cheese
½ cup finely chopped green bell pepper
2 teaspoons grated fresh onion
½ (8-ounce) block ⅓-less-fat cream cheese
    (Neufchâtel), softened
½ (8-ounce) block fat-free cream cheese,
    softened
⅔ cup chopped fresh parsley

1. Pat drained pineapple with paper towels to remove excess moisture. Combine pineapple and next 5 ingredients in a bowl; stir well. Cover and chill at least 30 minutes.

2. Shape cheese mixture into a ball. Press chopped parsley into ball, coating thoroughly. Cover and chill. Serve with reduced-fat crackers. Yield: 18 servings (serving size: about 1½ tablespoons).

Note: Our taste-testing panel enjoyed this cheesy spread served on melba toast and reduced-fat wheat crackers.

POINTS: 1; **Exchanges:** ½ Very Lean Meat, 1 Fat
Per serving: CAL 62 (46% from fat); PRO 4.5g; FAT 3.2g (sat 0g); CARB 3.5g; FIB 0.3g; CHOL 14mg; IRON 0.2mg; SOD 160mg; CALC 84mg

Mock Guacamole

2 cups frozen green peas, thawed
½ cup sliced green onions
2 tablespoons coarsely chopped fresh
    cilantro
1½ tablespoons fresh lime juice
1 tablespoon salsa
¼ teaspoon salt
¼ teaspoon hot sauce

1. Place first 4 ingredients in a food processor; process 30 seconds or until smooth, scraping sides of processor bowl once. Add remaining ingredients; pulse until blended. Serve with fat-free tortilla chips or raw vegetables. Yield: 24 servings (serving size: ¼ cup).

POINTS: 0; **Exchanges:** Free
Per serving: CAL 11 (0% from fat); PRO 0.7g; FAT 0g (sat 0g); CARB 1.9g; FIB 0.6g; CHOL 0mg; IRON 0.2mg; SOD 44mg; CALC 4mg

Fresh Fruit Dip

This dip is so thick and creamy it can double as a yummy spread for quick breads. If you prefer a thinner dip, add a small amount of juice from the crushed pineapple.

1   (8-ounce) tub light cream cheese, softened
1   (7-ounce) jar marshmallow creme
½   cup drained canned crushed pineapple in juice
1   teaspoon grated orange rind
½   teaspoon triple sec (orange-flavored liqueur)
⅛   teaspoon ground ginger

1. Combine all ingredients in a small bowl; stir well. Cover and chill. Serve with fresh fruit. Yield: 32 servings (serving size: 1 tablespoon).

POINTS: 1; **Exchanges:** ½ Starch
Per serving: CAL 39 (28% from fat); PRO 0.8g; FAT 1.2g (sat 0.7g); CARB 6.3g; FIB 0g; CHOL 4mg; IRON 0mg; SOD 42mg; CALC 10mg

Potato Skins With Cheese and Bacon is a low-fat rendition of a popular restaurant offering.

Potato Skins With Cheese and Bacon

Use the reserved potato pulp to make mashed potatoes.

4   medium baking potatoes (about 2 pounds)
Cooking spray
4   turkey-bacon slices
¾   cup (3 ounces) shredded reduced-fat sharp cheddar cheese
¼   cup fat-free sour cream
1   tablespoon minced fresh chives or finely chopped green onion

1. Preheat oven to 425°.

2. Bake potatoes at 425° for 1 hour or until tender. Cut each potato in half lengthwise; let cool slightly. Scoop out potato pulp, leaving a ¼-inch-thick shell. Reserve pulp for another use.

3. Place potato shells on a baking sheet. Spray inside of shells with cooking spray, and bake at

425° for 8 minutes or until crisp; set shells aside.

4. Cook bacon according to the package directions, and let cool slightly. Chop cooked bacon; set aside.

5. Sprinkle cheese evenly in potato shells. Bake at 425° for 5 minutes or until cheese melts. Sprinkle bacon evenly over cheese; top each serving with sour cream and chives. Yield: 8 servings.

POINTS: 2; **Exchanges:** 1 Starch, ½ Med-fat Meat
Per serving: CAL 106 (29% from fat); PRO 6.4g; FAT 3.4g (sat 1.6g); CARB 12.7g; FIB 1.1g; CHOL 12mg; IRON 0.9mg; SOD 182mg; CALC 104mg

Marinated Mushrooms

Cooking spray
2   tablespoons minced garlic
½   cup water
⅓   cup red wine vinegar
1½ tablespoons coriander seeds
¾   teaspoon dried thyme
¾   teaspoon dried oregano
½   teaspoon salt
½   teaspoon pepper
1½ pounds fresh mushrooms

1. Coat a large nonstick skillet with cooking spray; place over medium heat until hot. Add garlic; sauté 2 minutes. Add water and next 6 ingredients; bring to a boil. Stir in mushrooms. Cover, reduce heat to low, and cook 20 minutes or until mushrooms are tender, stirring occasionally.

2. Spoon mushroom mixture into a bowl; let cool completely. Cover and chill at least 8 hours. Drain mushrooms; discard marinade. Yield: 12 servings (serving size: ¼ cup).

POINTS: 0; **Exchanges:** Free
Per serving: CAL 20 (18% from fat); PRO 1.4g; FAT 0.4g (sat 0.1g); CARB 3.9g; FIB 1g; CHOL 0mg; IRON 1mg; SOD 101mg; CALC 14mg

Peanut Butter-Granola Gorp

For a quick, on-the-go snack, store this crunchy trail mix in small zip-top plastic bags.

1   cup low-fat granola with raisins (such as Kellogg's)
32 tiny fat-free pretzels, broken into small pieces
¼   cup creamy peanut butter
¼   cup maple-flavored pancake syrup

Cooking spray
½   cup golden raisins
½   cup dried sweetened cranberries (such as Craisins)

1. Preheat oven to 300°.

2. Place granola and pretzels in a large bowl; set aside. Combine peanut butter and syrup in a small microwave-safe bowl. Microwave at HIGH 30 seconds or until hot; stir well. Pour peanut butter mixture over granola mixture, stirring to coat. Spread mixture in a single layer on a jelly-roll pan coated with cooking spray.

3. Bake at 300° for 25 minutes, stirring every 8 minutes. Stir in raisins and cranberries; return pan to oven. Turn oven off; let mixture cool in closed oven 30 minutes. Remove from oven; let cool completely. Yield: 7 servings (serving size: ½ cup).

POINTS: 4; **Exchanges:** 2 Starch, 1 Fruit, ½ Med-fat Meat
Per serving: CAL 225 (23% from fat); PRO 5.1g; FAT 5.7g (sat 0.8g); CARB 42g; FIB 2.7g; CHOL 0mg; IRON 1.6mg; SOD 180mg; CALC 22mg

With dried cranberries and golden raisins, Peanut Butter-Granola Gorp satisfies the sweet tooth.

Quick Chicken Quesadilla Wedges

Leave the seeds in the jalapeño pepper if you prefer fiery food.

1   (10-ounce) can chunk white chicken in water, drained and flaked
1½ cups fat-free cottage cheese
2   tablespoons seeded chopped jalapeño pepper
8   (8-inch) fat-free flour tortillas
¾   cup (3 ounces) shredded reduced-fat Monterey Jack cheese
⅔   cup sliced green onions
1   cup chunky salsa
Cilantro sprigs (optional)

1. Preheat oven to 350°.
2. Combine first 3 ingredients in a bowl; stir well. Place 4 tortillas on an ungreased baking sheet; spoon chicken mixture evenly over each tortilla. Sprinkle cheese and green onions evenly over chicken mixture; top with remaining 4 tortillas.
3. Bake at 350° for 8 minutes or until warm. Cut each quesadilla into 6 wedges. Serve immediately with salsa. Garnish with cilantro sprigs, if desired. Yield: 24 servings (serving size: 1 quesadilla wedge and 2 teaspoons salsa).

POINTS: 1; **Exchanges:** 1 Very Lean Meat, ½ Starch
Per serving: CAL 73 (13% from fat); PRO 6.6g; FAT 1.1g (sat 0.7g); CARB 9.3g; FIB 0.3g; CHOL 3mg; IRON 0.3mg; SOD 268mg; CALC 45mg

Hummus Spread

This Middle Eastern bean purée is usually served with pita bread, but it's also delicious with zero-*POINT* carrot sticks, cucumber slices, and bell pepper strips.

½   cup 1% low-fat cottage cheese
2   tablespoons tahini (sesame-seed paste)
¼   teaspoon grated lemon rind
1   tablespoon fresh lemon juice
½   teaspoon ground coriander
⅛   teaspoon salt
1   garlic clove, peeled
1   (15-ounce) can chickpeas (garbanzo beans), drained
¼   cup minced fresh parsley

1. Place first 8 ingredients in a food processor; process until smooth, scraping sides of bowl once. Refrigerate in an airtight container. Sprinkle with parsley. Serve with pita bread or fresh vegetables. Yield: 4 servings (serving size: ½ cup).

POINTS: 4; **Exchanges:** 1½ Starch, 1 Very Lean Meat, ½ Fat
Per serving: CAL 184 (30% from fat); PRO 11.2g; FAT 6.1g (sat 0.9g); CARB 22.7g; FIB 3.4g; CHOL 1mg; IRON 3mg; SOD 342mg; CALC 92mg

Mini Garlic Pizzas

4   ounces block-style fat-free cream cheese (about ½ cup), softened
2   teaspoons minced fresh basil
1   teaspoon bottled minced roasted garlic
¼   cup grated Parmesan cheese, divided
10 (½-inch-thick) slices thin French bread baguette, toasted
1   large plum tomato, cut into 10 slices

1. Combine first 3 ingredients in a small bowl. Stir in 3 tablespoons Parmesan cheese. Spread 1 tablespoon cheese mixture over one side of each bread slice; top each with a tomato slice. Sprinkle remaining 1 tablespoon Parmesan cheese evenly over pizzas. Yield: 10 servings.

POINTS: 1; **Exchanges:** ½ Starch
Per serving: CAL 39 (23% from fat); PRO 3.1g; FAT 1g (sat 0.5g); CARB 4.5g; FIB 0.3g; CHOL 2mg; IRON 0.2mg; SOD 137mg; CALC 54mg

Pumpkin Dip

Close your eyes when you taste this dip and you'll think you're eating pumpkin pie.

2   (8-ounce) tubs light cream cheese, softened
1   (16-ounce) package powdered sugar, sifted
1   (16-ounce) can unsweetened pumpkin
2   teaspoons ground cinnamon
½   teaspoon ground nutmeg
2½   (1-pound) boxes gingersnaps (such as Nabisco)

1. Combine first 5 ingredients in a large bowl, and stir with a whisk until well blended. Serve immediately, or cover and chill. Serve dip with gingersnaps. Yield: 80 servings (serving size: 1 tablespoon dip and 2 gingersnaps).

POINTS: 2; **Exchanges:** 1 Starch, ½ Fat
Per serving: CAL 108 (30% from fat); PRO 1.7g; FAT 3.6g (sat 1.2g); CARB 17.3g; FIB 0.3g; CHOL 9mg; IRON 0.9mg; SOD 54mg; CALC 38 mg

All-Time-Favorite Desserts

ADD THESE TRIED-AND-TRUE SWEETS TO YOUR PERMANENT RECIPE FILE.

W*hether your tastes run to decadent delights such as Chocolate Éclair Icebox Dessert (page 91) and Mocha-Chocolate Trifle (page 82) or to homemade simplicity such as Chewy Chocolate Chip Cookies (page 93) and Peach Cobbler (page 90), you can't lose when you make any of these spectacular desserts. And although it will never occur to anyone as they bite into, say, our Fudgy Chocolate Brownies (page 92), all of these desserts not only garnered top grades from our panel of persnickety judges, but also met our nutritional requirements. We consider them to be true culinary magic.*

Store the dough for Peanut Butter Icebox Cookies in the freezer; then slice and bake a few cookies at a time.

Peanut Brittle-Apple Crisp

Peanut Butter Icebox Cookies

1   cup all-purpose flour
¼   teaspoon baking soda
⅛   teaspoon salt
3   tablespoons stick margarine, softened
2   tablespoons chunky peanut butter
½   cup firmly packed brown sugar
¼   cup granulated sugar
1   teaspoon vanilla extract
1   large egg white
Cooking spray

1. Combine first 3 ingredients in a bowl; stir well, and set aside.

2. Combine margarine and peanut butter in a large bowl; beat at medium speed of a mixer until light and fluffy. Gradually add sugars, beating at medium speed until well blended. Add vanilla and egg white; beat well. Stir in flour mixture. Turn dough out onto wax paper; shape into a 6-inch log. Wrap log in wax paper; freeze 3 hours.

3. Preheat oven to 350°.

4. Cut log into 24 (¼-inch-thick) slices. Place slices 1 inch apart on a baking sheets coated with cooking spray. Bake at 350° for 8 minutes. Remove cookies from pans, and let cool on wire racks. Yield: 2 dozen (serving size: 1 cookie).

POINTS: 2; **Exchanges:** ½ Starch, ½ Fat
Per serving: CAL 69 (31% from fat); PRO 1.2g; FAT 2.4g (sat 0.4g); CARB 10.8g; FIB 0.2g; CHOL 9mg; IRON 0.4mg; SOD 53mg; CALC 7mg

Peanut Brittle-Apple Crisp

½   cup all-purpose flour
¼   cup granulated sugar
¼   cup firmly packed brown sugar
⅛   teaspoon salt
¼   cup chilled butter or stick margarine, cut into small pieces
½   cup coarsely broken peanut brittle (about 2 ounces)
7   cups peeled sliced cooking apple (about 2 pounds)
3   tablespoons orange marmalade
2   cups vanilla low-fat frozen yogurt

1. Preheat oven to 375°.

2. Combine flour, sugars, and salt in a bowl; cut in margarine with a pastry blender or 2 knives

until mixture resembles coarse meal. Add peanut brittle; toss well.

3. Arrange apple slices in an 8-inch square baking dish; spoon marmalade over apple. Sprinkle flour mixture over marmalade. Bake at 375° for 40 minutes. Serve warm with yogurt. Yield: 8 servings (serving size: ⅓ cup crisp and ¼ cup yogurt).

POINTS: 6; **Exchanges:** 3½ Starch
Per serving: CAL 281 (25% from fat); PRO 2.9g; FAT 7.8g (sat 2g); CARB 53g; FIB 3.2g; CHOL 5mg; IRON 0.8mg; SOD 131mg; CALC 69mg

Spanish Flan

Flan is a Spanish baked custard with a caramelized sugar glaze. This one is topped with fresh strawberry halves, but any of your favorite berries may be substituted.

½   cup sugar, divided
Cooking spray
½   cup skim milk
1   (12-ounce) can evaporated skim milk
¾   cup egg substitute
½   teaspoon almond extract
⅛   teaspoon salt
2   cups fresh strawberry halves

1. Preheat oven to 325°.

2. Place ¼ cup sugar in a small heavy saucepan over medium-high heat; cook until sugar dissolves, stirring frequently. Continue cooking an additional 5 minutes or until golden, stirring constantly. Immediately pour caramelized sugar evenly into 6 (6-ounce) custard cups coated with cooking spray, tipping quickly until caramelized sugar coats bottoms of cups. Set aside.

3. Combine milks in a medium saucepan; cook over medium heat until thoroughly heated, stirring constantly.

4. Combine remaining ¼ cup sugar, egg substitute, almond extract, and salt in a medium bowl; beat at medium speed of a mixer until well blended. Gradually stir 1 cup hot milk into egg substitute mixture, and add to remaining hot milk, stirring constantly. Pour evenly into prepared custard cups.

5. Place custard cups in a 13- x 9-inch baking

pan, and add hot water to pan to depth of 1 inch. Bake at 325° for 50 minutes or until a knife inserted near center comes out clean. Remove cups from pan, and discard water. Let custards cool completely on a wire rack. Cover and chill at least 4 hours.

6. Loosen edges of custards with a knife or rubber spatula. Place a dessert plate, upside down, on top of each cup; invert custards onto plates. Top each custard with ⅓ cup fresh strawberry halves. Yield: 6 servings.

POINTS: 3; **Exchanges:** 1½ Starch, ½ Sk Milk
Per serving: CAL 148 (2% from fat); PRO 8.3g; FAT 0.4g (sat 0.1g); CARB 28.5g; FIB 1.3g; CHOL 3mg; IRON 0.9mg; SOD 170mg; CALC 207mg

Black Bottom Banana-Cream Pie

Pastry Crust
3   tablespoons cornstarch, divided
2   tablespoons sugar
2   tablespoons unsweetened cocoa
Dash of salt
1⅓ cups 1% low-fat milk, divided
1   ounce semisweet chocolate, chopped
½   cup sugar
1   tablespoon butter or stick margarine
¼   teaspoon salt
2   large eggs
2   teaspoons vanilla extract
2   ounces block-style fat-free cream cheese (about ¼ cup), softened
2   cups sliced ripe banana (about 2 large bananas)
1½ cups frozen fat-free whipped topping, thawed
Chocolate curls (optional)

1. Prepare and bake Pastry Crust. Let cool completely on a wire rack.

2. Combine 1 tablespoon cornstarch, 2 tablespoons sugar, cocoa, and dash of salt in a small heavy saucepan; gradually add ⅓ cup milk, stirring with a whisk. Cook 2 minutes over medium-low heat. Stir in chocolate; bring to a boil over medium heat. Reduce heat to low; cook 1 minute, stirring constantly. Spread chocolate mixture into bottom of prepared crust.

3. Combine remaining 2 tablespoons cornstarch,

½ cup sugar, butter, and ¼ teaspoon salt in a heavy saucepan. Stir in remaining 1 cup milk and eggs; bring to a boil over medium heat, stirring constantly with a whisk. Reduce heat to low, and cook 30 seconds or until thick. Remove from heat; stir in vanilla.

4. Place cream cheese in a large bowl; beat at medium speed of a mixer 30 seconds. Add ¼ cup hot custard to cream cheese, beating just until blended. Gradually stir in remaining hot custard.

5. Arrange banana slices on top of chocolate layer in prepared crust; spoon custard over bananas. Cover surface of filling with plastic wrap; chill 4 hours. Remove plastic wrap. Spread whipped topping evenly over custard. Garnish with chocolate curls, if desired. Chill until ready to serve. Yield: 8 servings.

POINTS: 7; **Exchanges:** 3 Starch, 1½ Fat
Per serving: CAL 315 (29% from fat); PRO 6.9g; FAT 10.1g (sat 4.8g); CARB 49.6g; FIB 1.6g; CHOL 58mg; IRON 1.4mg; SOD 253mg; CALC 94mg

Pastry Crust:

1   cup all-purpose flour, divided
3   tablespoons ice water
½   teaspoon cider vinegar
1   tablespoon powdered sugar
¼   teaspoon salt
¼   cup vegetable shortening

1. Preheat oven to 400°.

2. Combine ¼ cup flour, ice water, and vinegar, stirring with a whisk until well blended.

3. Combine ¾ cup flour, sugar, and salt in a bowl; cut in shortening with a pastry blender or 2 knives until mixture resembles coarse meal. Add ice water mixture; toss with a fork until moist. Gently press mixture into a 4-inch circle on heavy-duty plastic wrap; cover with additional plastic wrap. Roll dough, still covered, into a 12-inch circle; chill 15 minutes. Remove plastic wrap; fit dough into a 9-inch pie plate. Press the dough against bottom and sides of pan. Fold edges under; flute. Pierce bottom and sides of dough with a fork; bake at 400° for 20 minutes or until edge is lightly browned. Let cool on a wire rack. Yield: 1 (9-inch) crust.

Food Processor Variation:

1. Preheat oven to 400°.

2. Place 1 cup flour, sugar, and salt in a food processor, and pulse 2 times or until combined. Add shortening, and pulse 10 times or until mixture is combined. Add ice water and vinegar through food chute, pulsing just until combined (do not form a ball).

3. Gently press mixture into a 4-inch circle on heavy-duty plastic wrap, and proceed with recipe as directed above.

Old-fashioned Spice Cake

Cooking spray
1   tablespoon cake flour
¾   cup granulated sugar
¼   cup butter or stick margarine, softened
2   tablespoons vegetable oil
2½   teaspoons vanilla extract
½   cup firmly packed brown sugar
⅓   cup plain fat-free yogurt
2   large egg whites
3   cups sifted cake flour
1¾   teaspoons baking powder
1   teaspoon ground cinnamon
¾   teaspoon ground allspice
½   teaspoon baking soda
½   teaspoon ground nutmeg
1½   cups skim milk
Caramel Frosting

1. Preheat oven to 350°.

2. Coat 3 (8-inch) round cake pans with cooking spray; dust with 1 tablespoon flour.

3. Beat granulated sugar, butter, oil, and vanilla at medium speed of a mixer for 1½ minutes or until well blended. Add brown sugar, yogurt, and egg whites; beat at high speed of a mixer 1½ minutes.

4. Combine sifted cake flour and next 5 ingredients in a bowl; stir well. Add flour mixture to creamed mixture alternately with milk, beginning and ending with flour mixture.

5. Pour batter into prepared pans. Sharply tap

pans once on counter to remove air bubbles. Bake at 350° for 24 minutes or until a wooden pick inserted in center comes out clean. Let cool in pans 10 minutes on wire racks; remove from pans. Let cool completely on wire racks.

6. Place 1 cake layer on a plate. Spread ⅓ cup Caramel Frosting over top of layer, and top with another cake layer. Spread ⅓ cup frosting over top of layer, and top with remaining cake layer. Spread remaining frosting over top and sides of cake. Yield: 16 servings.

POINTS: 7; **Exchanges:** 4 Starch, ½ Fat
Per serving: CAL 331 (18% from fat); PRO 3.9g; FAT 6.7g (sat 3.3g); CARB 64.2g; FIB 0.1g; CHOL 14mg; IRON 2.1mg; SOD 82mg; CALC 116mg

Caramel Frosting:

1   cup firmly packed brown sugar
½   cup evaporated skim milk
2½   tablespoons butter or stick margarine
2   teaspoons light-colored corn syrup
Dash of salt
2   cups powdered sugar
2½   teaspoons vanilla extract
1½   teaspoons evaporated skim milk (optional)

Bananas drenched in creamy custard fill a chocolate-coated crust in Black Bottom Banana-Cream Pie.

Chopped toffee bars add a satisfying crunch to Mocha-Chocolate Trifle.

1. Combine first 5 ingredients in a medium saucepan; bring to a boil over medium-high heat. Reduce heat, and simmer 5 minutes or until thick and golden brown. Remove from heat. Add powdered sugar and vanilla; beat at medium speed of a mixer until smooth and slightly warm. Add 1½ teaspoons milk, ½ teaspoon at a time, for a more spreadable consistency, if needed. Yield: 1¾ cups.

Mocha-Chocolate Trifle

This spectacular dessert serves a crowd and can be made ahead of time.

1   (18.25-ounce) package light devil's food cake mix
1⅓ cups water
2   tablespoons vegetable oil
2   large egg whites
1   large egg
Cooking spray
3   cups cold skim milk
1   (3.9-ounce) package chocolate instant pudding mix (do not substitute sugar-free or fat-free)
½   cup Kahlúa (coffee-flavored liqueur) or ½ cup strong brewed coffee
1   (8-ounce) carton frozen fat-free whipped topping, thawed
½   cup chopped reduced-fat chocolate toffee crisp bars (about 4 bars) (such as Hershey's Sweet Escapes)

1. Preheat oven to 350°.

2. Combine first 5 ingredients in a large bowl; beat at medium speed of a mixer until well blended. Spoon batter into a 13- x 9-inch baking pan coated with cooking spray. Bake at 350° for 25 minutes or until a wooden pick inserted in center comes out clean. Let cool in pan 10 minutes on a wire rack; remove from pan. Let cool completely on a wire rack.

3. Combine milk and pudding mix in a medium bowl; prepare according to package directions.

4. Tear cake into bite-size pieces. Place half of cake pieces in a 3-quart clear, glass bowl or trifle dish. Pour half of Kahlúa over cake pieces, and top with half of pudding, half of whipped topping, and half of chocolate bars. Repeat procedure with remaining cake, Kahlúa, pudding, whipped topping, and chocolate bars. Cover and chill at least 4 hours. Yield: 16 servings (serving size: about 1 cup).

POINTS: 5; **Exchanges:** 3 Starch, ½ Fat
Per serving: CAL 269 (14% from fat); PRO 4.1g; FAT 4.2g (sat 1.3g); CARB 48.4g; FIB 1.1g; CHOL 16mg; IRON 1mg; SOD 476mg; CALC 93mg

Bittersweet Chocolate Pudding

3½ cups skim milk, divided
1   cup Dutch process or unsweetened cocoa
3   tablespoons cornstarch
¼   teaspoon salt
1   cup sugar
1   large egg
1   large egg yolk
2   ounces bittersweet chocolate, coarsely chopped
1   tablespoon vanilla extract

1. Combine 1 cup skim milk, cocoa, cornstarch, and salt in a large bowl; stir well with a whisk. Set aside.

2. Cook remaining 2½ cups skim milk in a large, heavy saucepan over medium-high heat to 180° or until tiny bubbles form around edge (do not boil). Remove from heat; add sugar, stirring with a whisk until sugar dissolves. Stir in cocoa mixture. Bring to a boil over medium heat, and cook 2 minutes, stirring constantly.

3. Combine egg and egg yolk in a bowl; stir well

EDITOR'S CHOICE

with a whisk. Gradually add hot milk mixture to egg mixture, stirring constantly. Return mixture to pan. Cook over medium heat 2 minutes or until thick, stirring constantly. Remove from heat; add chocolate and vanilla, stirring until chocolate melts. Pour ½ cup pudding into each of 8 small bowls. Serve warm or chilled. Yield: 8 servings (serving size: ½ cup).

POINTS: 5; **Exchanges:** 2½ Starch, ½ Sk Milk, ½ Fat
Per serving: CAL 249 (18% from fat); PRO 8.3g; FAT 5.1g (sat 2.7g); CARB 43g; FIB 0g; CHOL 57mg; IRON 2.3mg; SOD 144mg; CALC 157mg

Blueberry Pound Cake

If you're using frozen blueberries, do not thaw them before adding them to the batter.

2   cups granulated sugar
½   cup light butter (such as Land O' Lakes)
½   cup (4 ounces) ⅓-less-fat cream cheese (Neufchâtel), softened
3   large eggs
1   large egg white
3   cups all-purpose flour, divided
2   cups fresh or frozen blueberries
1   teaspoon baking powder
½   teaspoon baking soda
½   teaspoon salt
1   (8-ounce) carton lemon low-fat yogurt
2   teaspoons vanilla extract
Cooking spray
½   cup powdered sugar
4   teaspoons lemon juice

1. Preheat oven to 350°.

2. Combine first 3 ingredients in a large bowl; beat at medium speed of a mixer 5 minutes or until well blended. Add eggs and egg white, 1 at a time, beating well after each addition. Combine 2 tablespoons flour and blueberries in a small bowl, and toss well. Combine remaining flour, baking powder, baking soda, and salt in a medium bowl; stir well. Add flour mixture to sugar mixture alternately with yogurt, beginning and ending with flour mixture. Fold in blueberry mixture and vanilla.

3. Pour batter into a 10-inch tube pan coated with cooking spray. Bake at 350° for 1 hour and 10 minutes or until a wooden pick inserted in center comes out clean. Let cool in pan 10 minutes on a wire rack; remove from pan.

4. Combine powdered sugar and lemon juice in a small bowl; stir well. Drizzle over warm cake. Cut with a serrated knife. Yield: 16 servings.

POINTS: 6; **Exchanges:** 3½ Starch, ½ Fat
Per serving: CAL 287 (19% from fat); PRO 5.7g; FAT 6.1g (sat 3.4g); CARB 53.9g; FIB 1.5g; CHOL 57mg; IRON 1.3mg; SOD 227mg; CALC 50mg

Strawberry Snack Cake

1½   cups all-purpose flour
½   cup sugar
2   teaspoons baking powder
⅛   teaspoon salt
½   cup strawberry low-fat yogurt
¼   cup skim milk
3   tablespoons stick margarine, melted
½   teaspoon vanilla extract
1   large egg, lightly beaten
⅔   cup sliced strawberries, slightly mashed
Cooking spray
1   teaspoon powdered sugar

1. Preheat oven to 350°.

2. Combine first 4 ingredients in a large bowl; stir well, and make a well in center of mixture. Combine yogurt and next 4 ingredients in a bowl; stir well. Add to flour mixture, stirring just until moist. Gently fold in mashed strawberries.

3. Spoon batter into an 8-inch square baking pan coated with cooking spray. Bake at 350° for 25

Blueberry Pound Cake doubles as a dessert and a sweet breakfast bread.

minutes or until a wooden pick inserted in center comes out clean. Let cake cool in pan at least 10 minutes on a wire rack. Serve warm or at room temperature. Sift powdered sugar over cake just before serving. Yield: 9 servings.

POINTS: 4; **Exchanges**: 2 Starch, 1 Fat
Per serving: CAL 183 (24% from fat); PRO 3.7g; FAT 4.8g (sat 1.1g); CARB 31.3g; FIB 0.9g; CHOL 25mg; SOD 95mg; IRON 1.2mg; CALC 95mg

Brown Sugar Angel Food Cake

Words such as "wonderful," "fabulous," and "I'd make this at home" echoed at the testing table when we tried this. We think you'll agree with our rave reviews.

2   cups firmly packed brown sugar, divided
1¼ cups sifted cake flour
12 large egg whites (at room temperature)
1½ teaspoons cream of tartar
1   teaspoon salt
2   teaspoons vanilla extract
1   tablespoon powdered sugar

1. Preheat oven to 350°.

2. Sift 1 cup brown sugar and cake flour together into a small bowl; set aside.

3. Beat egg whites with clean, dry beaters at high speed of a mixer until foamy. Add cream of tartar and salt, and beat until soft peaks form. Add remaining 1 cup brown sugar, 2 tablespoons at a time, beating until stiff peaks form and brown sugar dissolves. Sift flour mixture over egg whites, ¼ cup at a time, folding in after each addition. Fold in vanilla.

4. Spoon batter into an ungreased 10-inch tube pan. Break air pockets by cutting through batter with a knife. Bake at 350° for 50 minutes or until cake springs back when touched lightly in center.

5. Remove cake from oven; invert pan, and let cake cool completely upside-down in pan. Loosen cake from sides of pan using a long narrow metal spatula; remove from pan. Sprinkle powdered sugar evenly over top of cake. Yield: 10 servings.

POINTS: 5; **Exchanges**: 3½ Starch
Per serving: CAL 241 (0% from fat); PRO 5.2g; FAT 0.1g (sat 0g); CARB 55g; FIB 0g; CHOL 0mg; IRON 1.9mg; SOD 315mg; CALC 42mg

Strawberry-Buttermilk Ice Cream

Strawberry extract enhances the flavor of this recipe, but it can be omitted.

2¼ cups fresh strawberries
½ cup sugar
¼ cup thawed orange juice concentrate, undiluted
2   teaspoons vanilla extract
1   teaspoon imitation strawberry extract (optional)
1   large ripe banana
2   cups low-fat buttermilk
Orange rind strips (optional)

1. Place first 6 ingredients in a food processor; process until smooth. Combine strawberry mixture and buttermilk in freezer can of an ice-cream freezer, and freeze according to manufacturer's instructions. Spoon ice cream into a freezer-safe container; cover and freeze 1 hour or until firm. Garnish with orange rind strips, if desired. Yield: 11 servings (serving size: ½ cup).

POINTS: 2; **Exchanges**: 1 Starch
Per serving: CAL 94 (9% from fat); PRO 2.1g; FAT 0.9g (sat 0.5g); CARB 19.7g; FIB 1.3g; CHOL 0mg; IRON 0.2mg; SOD 24mg; CALC 62mg

Coconut Cream Pie

1   cup vanilla wafer crumbs (about 26 wafers)
2   tablespoons reduced-calorie stick margarine, melted
Cooking spray
2   large egg yolks, lightly beaten
6   tablespoons sugar
3   tablespoons cornstarch
¼ teaspoon salt
2½ cups skim milk
½ cup flaked sweetened coconut
1   teaspoon vanilla extract
½ teaspoon imitation coconut extract
3   large egg whites (at room temperature)
3   tablespoons sugar
1   tablespoon flaked sweetened coconut

1. Preheat oven to 350°.

2. Combine crumbs and margarine in a bowl; stir well. Press into bottom and up sides of a 9-inch pie plate coated with cooking spray. Bake at 350° for 10 minutes; let cool on a wire rack. Reduce

Strawberry-Buttermilk Ice Cream

Berry-Lemon Pudding Cake is a light dessert that complements a hearty meal.

oven temperature to 325°.

3. Place egg yolks in a bowl; stir well, and set aside. Combine 6 tablespoons sugar, cornstarch, and salt in a medium saucepan. Gradually add milk, stirring with a whisk until well blended. Bring to a boil over medium heat; cook 1 minute, stirring constantly with a whisk. Remove from heat.

4. Gradually stir one-fourth of hot milk mixture into yolks, and add to remaining hot milk mixture, stirring constantly. Cook over medium heat 2 minutes or until mixture is thick, stirring constantly. Remove from heat; stir in ½ cup coconut, vanilla, and coconut extract. Pour into prepared crust, and set aside.

5. Beat egg whites with clean, dry beaters at high speed of a mixer until foamy. Gradually add 3 tablespoons sugar, 1 tablespoon at a time, beating until stiff peaks form and sugar dissolves.

6. Spread egg white mixture over hot filling,

sealing to edge of crust. Sprinkle with 1 tablespoon coconut. Bake at 325° for 25 minutes or until golden. Let cool completely on a wire rack. Store any leftover pie loosely covered in the refrigerator. Yield: 9 servings.

POINTS: 5; **Exchanges:** 2 Starch, 1 Fat
Per serving: CAL 220 (36% from fat); PRO 4.9g; FAT 8.8g (sat 3.5g); CARB 29.9g; FIB 0.3g; CHOL 50mg; IRON 0.5mg; SOD 219mg; CALC 97mg

Nectarine-Daiquiri Sorbet

Leave the skins on the nectarines for added flecks of color.

2   cups water
1   cup sugar
4   cups sliced fresh nectarines (about 1½ pounds)
½   cup fresh lime juice
½   cup white rum

1. Combine water and sugar in a saucepan; cook over medium heat, stirring until sugar dissolves.

Remove from heat, and let cool completely.

2. Place nectarines, lime juice, and rum in a food processor; process until smooth. Spoon nectarine mixture into a bowl; stir in sugar syrup.

3. Pour mixture into freezer can of an ice cream freezer, and freeze according to manufacturer's instructions. Spoon into a freezer-safe container; freeze 1 hour or until firm. Yield: 16 servings (serving size: ½ cup).

POINTS: 2; **Exchanges:** 1 Starch
Per serving: CAL 83 (2% from fat); PRO 0.3g; FAT 0.2g (sat 0g); CARB 17.2g; FIB 0.8g; CHOL 0mg; IRON 0.1mg; SOD 0mg; CALC 2mg

Berry-Lemon Pudding Cake

As this fruity dessert bakes, a delicate sponge cake forms over a creamy bottom layer of custard. The water bath cooks this pudding cake with gentle, even heat.

⅔ cup granulated sugar
¼ cup all-purpose flour
⅛ teaspoon salt
⅛ teaspoon ground nutmeg
1 cup low-fat buttermilk
1 teaspoon grated lemon rind
¼ cup fresh lemon juice
2 tablespoons butter or stick margarine, melted
2 large egg yolks
3 large egg whites (at room temperature)
¼ cup granulated sugar
1½ cups fresh blackberries, blueberries, or raspberries
Cooking spray
¾ teaspoon powdered sugar

1. Preheat oven to 350°.

2. Combine first 4 ingredients in a large bowl. Combine buttermilk and next 4 ingredients in a bowl; stir well. Add to flour mixture, stirring with a whisk until smooth.

3. Beat egg whites with clean, dry beaters at high speed of a mixer until foamy. Add ¼ cup granulated sugar, 1 tablespoon at a time, beating until stiff peaks form. Gently stir one-fourth of egg white mixture into buttermilk mixture, and gently fold in remaining egg white mixture. Fold in berries.

4. Pour batter into an 8-inch square baking pan coated with cooking spray. Place in a larger baking pan; add hot water to larger pan to a depth of 1 inch. Bake at 350° for 35 minutes or until cake springs back when touched lightly in center. Sift powdered sugar over cake. Serve warm. Yield: 5 servings (serving size: 1 cup).

POINTS: 6; **Exchanges:** 3½ Starch, ½ Fat
Per serving: CAL 285 (23% from fat); PRO 6g; FAT 7.2g (sat 1.7g); CARB 51.2g; FIB 3.3g; CHOL 89mg; IRON 0.8mg; SOD 198mg; CALC 86mg

Banana-Coconut Crumb Cake

1¼ cups all-purpose flour
⅓ cup granulated sugar
⅓ cup firmly packed dark brown sugar
¼ teaspoon ground allspice
⅛ teaspoon salt
¼ cup chilled butter or stick margarine, cut into small pieces
¾ teaspoon baking powder
½ teaspoon baking soda
½ cup mashed ripe banana
3 tablespoons 1% low-fat milk
1 large egg
Cooking spray
¼ cup flaked sweetened coconut
1 teaspoon water

1. Preheat oven to 350°.

2. Combine first 5 ingredients in a bowl; cut in butter with a pastry blender or 2 knives until mixture resembles coarse meal. Reserve ½ cup flour mixture for topping, and set aside.

3. Combine remaining flour mixture, baking powder, and baking soda; add mashed banana, milk, and egg. Beat at medium speed of a mixer until blended. Spoon batter into an 8-inch round cake pan coated with cooking spray. Combine reserved ½ cup flour mixture, coconut, and water; stir with a fork. Sprinkle crumb mixture over batter. Bake at 350° for 30 minutes or until cake springs back when touched lightly in center. Let cool on a wire rack. Yield: 8 servings.

POINTS: 5; **Exchanges:** 2½ Starch, 1 Fat
Per serving: CAL 229 (31% from fat); PRO 3.3g; FAT 7.8g (sat 2.3g); CARB 37.3g; FIB 1.1g; CHOL 28mg; IRON 1.3mg; SOD 205mg; CALC 50mg

Apple Cider-Caramel Cake

Cider "syrup" is folded into this cake for a rich caramelized flavor.

2¼ cups apple cider, divided
2¼ cups granulated sugar, divided
1 tablespoon butter or stick margarine
3 cups peeled sliced cooking apple
6 tablespoons fresh lemon juice, divided
1 teaspoon vanilla extract
Cooking spray
2½ tablespoons dry breadcrumbs
½ cup butter or stick margarine, softened
1 tablespoon grated lemon rind
1 (8-ounce) block fat-free cream cheese
3 large eggs
3 cups all-purpose flour
½ teaspoon baking soda
¼ teaspoon salt
1 cup low-fat buttermilk
1 tablespoon powdered sugar

1. Bring 2 cups cider to a boil in a large, heavy saucepan over high heat. Cook 20 minutes or until reduced to ½ cup. Reduce heat to medium-high; stir in ½ cup granulated sugar. Cook 5 minutes or until sugar dissolves and cider is thick and dark-colored, stirring occasionally. Remove from heat; let cool 1 minute. Stir in 1 tablespoon butter. Stir in apple; cook 15 minutes over medium-high heat or until liquid is absorbed, stirring frequently. Remove from heat, and let cool. (If apple mixture hardens, place it over low heat until softened).

2. Preheat oven to 325°.

3. Combine ¼ cup cider, ¼ cup granulated sugar, ¼ cup lemon juice, and vanilla in a small bowl; set mixture aside, stirring occasionally until sugar dissolves.

4. Coat a 12-cup Bundt pan with cooking spray; dust with breadcrumbs.

5. Combine 1½ cups granulated sugar, ½ cup butter, lemon rind, and cream cheese in a large bowl; beat at medium speed of a mixer 5 minutes or until well blended. Add eggs, 1 at a time, beating well after each addition. Beat in 2 tablespoons lemon juice. Combine flour, baking soda, and salt. Add flour mixture to sugar mixture alternately with buttermilk, beginning and ending with flour mixture. Fold in apple mixture. Pour into prepared pan; bake at 325° for 1½ hours or until a wooden pick inserted in center comes out clean. Let cool in pan 5 minutes; pierce with a wooden skewer in several places. Pour cider mixture over cake in pan, and let stand 10 minutes. Remove from pan, and let cool completely on a wire rack. Sift powdered sugar over top of cake. Yield: 18 servings.

POINTS: 6; **Exchanges:** 3½ Starch, ½ Fat
Per serving: CAL 286 (22% from fat); PRO 5.8g; FAT 7.1g (sat 1.6g); CARB 50.1g; FIB 1.2g; CHOL 39mg; IRON 1.3mg; SOD 237mg; CALC 68mg

Hot Maple Soufflés

Be sure to use real maple syrup, not artificially flavored pancake syrup, in this recipe.

1 tablespoon butter or stick margarine, softened
2 tablespoons granulated sugar
3 tablespoons maple syrup
3 tablespoons bourbon
1 cup maple syrup
4 large egg whites (at room temperature)
⅛ teaspoon salt
1 teaspoon baking powder
1 tablespoon powdered sugar

1. Preheat oven to 425°.

2. Coat 6 (10-ounce) ramekins with margarine; sprinkle evenly with granulated sugar. Combine 3 tablespoons maple syrup and bourbon in a

Use crisp, fresh fall apples to make Apple Cider-Caramel Cake.

small microwave-safe bowl; microwave at HIGH 1½ minutes or until mixture boils. Pour about 1 tablespoon bourbon mixture into bottom of each prepared ramekin.

3. Cook 1 cup maple syrup in a medium, heavy saucepan over medium-high heat 8 minutes or until candy thermometer registers 250°. Beat egg whites and salt with clean, dry beaters at medium speed of a mixer until foamy. Pour hot maple syrup in a thin stream over egg whites, beating at medium speed and then at high speed until stiff peaks form. Add baking powder, and beat well. Spoon egg white mixture evenly into prepared ramekins; place on a jelly-roll pan. Bake at 425° for 13 minutes or until puffy and set. Sift powdered sugar evenly over tops of soufflés. Serve immediately. Yield: 6 servings.

POINTS: 4; **Exchanges:** 3 Starch
Per serving: CAL 212 (8% from fat); PRO 2.3g; FAT 2g (sat 0.4g); CARB 47.8g; FIB 0g; CHOL 0mg; IRON 0.8mg; SOD 193mg; CALC 89mg

Baked Apples With Cinnamon Ice Cream

1½ cups vanilla low-fat ice cream, softened
½   teaspoon ground cinnamon
6   small Rome apples
6   tablespoons brown sugar
¼   cup reduced-calorie stick margarine
2   tablespoons raisins
Ground cinnamon (optional)

1. Combine softened ice cream and ½ teaspoon cinnamon in a 9-inch square baking pan; stir well. Spread evenly in pan; cover and freeze 2 hours or until firm.

2. Core apples, cutting to, but not through, bottom of each apple. Spoon 1 tablespoon brown sugar, 2 teaspoons margarine, and 1 teaspoon raisins into center of each apple. Place apples in an 11- x 7-inch baking dish; cover with heavy-duty plastic wrap, and vent. Microwave at HIGH 10 minutes or until apples are tender, turning dish a half-turn after 5 minutes.

3. Place apples in individual serving dishes; driz-zle cooking liquid in baking dish evenly over apples. Top each apple with ¼ cup ice cream mixture. Sprinkle with cinnamon, if desired. Yield: 6 servings.

POINTS: 4; **Exchanges:** 1 Starch, 1½ Fruit, 1 Fat
Per serving: CAL 226 (27% from fat); PRO 1.7g; FAT 6.8g (sat 0.8g); CARB 43.7g; FIB 5.2g; CHOL 5mg; IRON 0.6mg; SOD 105mg; CALC 69mg

Honey-Grapefruit Granita

1   cup sugar
1   cup water
4   cups fresh pink grapefruit juice (about 10 large grapefruit)
⅓   cup honey

1. Combine sugar and water in a medium saucepan, and stir well. Bring to a boil, and cook 1 minute or until sugar dissolves, stirring constantly. Combine sugar syrup and grapefruit juice in a large bowl; stir well, and set aside.

Serve Hot Maple Soufflés with seasonal fresh fruit for an elegant ending to a special meal.

EDITOR'S CHOICE

Next time you need an easy make-ahead dessert, try Chocolate-Éclair Icebox Dessert.

2. Place honey in a small bowl. Microwave at HIGH 30 seconds or until warm. Add to juice mixture; stir well. Pour mixture into a 13- x 9-inch baking dish; cover and freeze at least 8 hours or until firm.

3. Remove mixture from freezer, and scrape entire mixture with the tines of a fork until fluffy. Spoon into a freezer-safe container; cover and freeze up to 1 month. Yield: 6 servings (serving size: 1 cup).

POINTS: 5; **Exchanges:** 4 Fruit
Per serving: CAL 248 (1% from fat); PRO 0.9g; FAT 0.2g (sat 0g); CARB 63.7g; FIB 0g; CHOL 0mg; IRON 3.4mg; SOD 2mg; CALC 13mg

Peach Cobbler

If fresh peaches are out of season, substitute the same amount of frozen peach slices. Just thaw them before you use them.

2 cups all-purpose flour
1 tablespoon sugar
¼ teaspoon salt
6 tablespoons chilled stick margarine, cut into 6 pieces
6 tablespoons ice water
Cooking spray
6 cups peeled sliced peaches (about 3¾ pounds)
¾ cup firmly packed brown sugar, divided
2½ tablespoons all-purpose flour
1 tablespoon vanilla extract
1 teaspoon ground cinnamon
¼ cup slivered almonds
1 large egg, lightly beaten
1 teaspoon water
1 tablespoon granulated sugar

1. Preheat oven to 375°.

2. Place first 3 ingredients in a food processor; pulse 2 or 3 times. Add chilled margarine, and pulse 10 times or until mixture resembles coarse meal. With processor on, slowly add ice water through food chute, processing just until combined (do not form a ball).

3. Gently press flour mixture into a 4-inch circle on heavy-duty plastic wrap; cover with additional plastic wrap. Roll dough, still covered, into a 15- x 13-inch rectangle. Chill dough 15 minutes or until plastic wrap can be easily removed. Remove plastic wrap, and fit dough into a 11- x 7-inch baking dish coated with cooking spray, allowing dough to extend over edges of dish.

4. Combine peaches, ½ cup brown sugar, 2½ tablespoons flour, vanilla, and cinnamon in a large bowl; toss gently. Spoon peach mixture into pastry dough; fold edges of dough over peach mixture (it will only partially cover peaches). Sprinkle remaining ¼ cup brown sugar over peach mixture; sprinkle with almonds.

5. Combine egg and 1 teaspoon water in a small bowl; stir well. Brush egg mixture over dough, and sprinkle with 1 tablespoon sugar. Bake at 375° for 45 minutes or until filling is bubbly and crust is lightly browned. Let stand 30 minutes before serving. Yield: 10 servings.

POINTS: 6; **Exchanges:** 3½ Starch, 1 Fat
Per serving: CAL 302 (27% from fat); PRO 4.5g; FAT 9.2g (sat 1.6g); CARB 51.5g; FIB 2.8g; CHOL 11mg; IRON 1.9mg; SOD 149mg; CALC 39mg

Peachy Ice Cream Desserts

2½ cups vanilla low-fat ice cream, softened
1½ cups frozen sliced peaches, thawed and coarsely chopped
2 teaspoons lemon juice
½ cup peach preserves
¼ cup amaretto (almond-flavored liqueur), divided
1 (11-ounce) package fat-free soft oatmeal-raisin cookies (such as Archway)

1. Combine first 3 ingredients in a large bowl, and stir well. Spread ice cream mixture into an 8-inch square baking pan. Cover and freeze 2 hours or until firm.

2. Combine peach preserves and 2 tablespoons amaretto in a small saucepan; cook over low heat until preserves melt, stirring constantly. Remove from heat; set aside, and keep warm.

3. Place 1 cookie in each of 10 (2½-inch) muffin cups. Firmly press cookies against bottoms and up sides of cups. Brush remaining 2 tablespoons

amaretto evenly over cookies; let stand 15 minutes. Remove cookie cups from pan, and place on individual dessert plates. Scoop ice cream mixture into cookie cups. Drizzle evenly with peach preserves mixture. Yield: 10 servings.

POINTS: 4; **Exchanges:** 2 Starch, 1½ Fruit
Per serving: CAL 239 (9% from fat); PRO 3.6g; FAT 2.5g (sat 0.1g); CARB 53.8g; FIB 3.3g; CHOL 0mg; IRON 0.9mg; SOD 126mg; CALC 64mg

Chocolate-Éclair Icebox Dessert

22½ sheets low-fat honey graham crackers (about 1 [14-ounce] box), divided
Cooking spray
3 cups cold skim milk
2 (3.4-ounce) packages vanilla fat-free instant pudding mix (do not substitute sugar-free)
1 (8-ounce) block fat-free cream cheese
1 (8-ounce) tub frozen reduced-calorie whipped topping, thawed
¼ cup skim milk
2 tablespoons butter or stick margarine, softened
2 tablespoons honey
2 ounces unsweetened chocolate, melted
1½ cups sifted powdered sugar

1. Arrange 7½ graham cracker sheets in bottom of a 13- x 9-inch baking dish coated with cooking spray. Combine 3 cups milk, pudding mix, and cream cheese in a large bowl; beat at low speed of a mixer 1 minute or until thick. Fold in whipped topping. Spread half of pudding mixture over graham crackers; top with 7½ graham cracker sheets. Repeat procedure with remaining half of pudding mixture and 7½ graham cracker sheets.

2. Combine ¼ cup milk, butter, honey, and unsweetened chocolate in a medium bowl; beat at medium speed of mixer until well blended. Gradually add powdered sugar, beating until well blended. Spread chocolate glaze over graham crackers. Cover dessert loosely by tenting with foil; chill 4 hours. Yield: 18 servings.

POINTS: 5; **Exchanges:** 2½ Starch, ½ Fat
Per serving: CAL 234 (22% from fat); PRO 5.4g; FAT 5.8g (sat 2.7g); CARB 41.5g; FIB 0.8g; CHOL 3mg; IRON 1mg; SOD 352mg; CALC 105mg

Crunchy Oat-Apricot Bars

Most any flavor of fruit preserves can be used in place of apricot.

2   cups regular oats
1¾ cups all-purpose flour
1   cup firmly packed brown sugar
⅔ cup reduced-calorie stick margarine
1½ teaspoons vanilla extract
Cooking spray
1½ cups apricot preserves

1. Preheat oven to 350°.

2. Place first 5 ingredients in a food processor; pulse 4 to 5 times or until oat mixture resembles coarse meal. Press half of oat mixture into bottom of a 13- x 9-inch baking pan coated with cooking spray. Spread apricot preserves over oat mixture. Sprinkle remaining oat mixture over preserves, pressing gently. Bake at 350° for 35 minutes or until bubbly and golden brown. Let cool completely in pan on a wire rack. Yield: 36 servings.

POINTS: 2; **Exchanges:** 1 Starch, ½ Fruit
Per serving: CAL 113 (20% from fat); PRO 1.4g; FAT 2.5g (sat 0.5g); CARB 22.2g; FIB 0.8g; CHOL 0mg; IRON 0.7mg; SOD 41mg; CALC 11mg

Lemon-Cornmeal Icebox Cookies

¾ cup all-purpose flour
¼ cup yellow cornmeal
¼ teaspoon baking soda
⅛ teaspoon salt
4   tablespoons stick margarine, softened
¾ cup sugar
2   teaspoons grated lemon rind
1   teaspoon vanilla extract
1   large egg white
Cooking spray

1. Combine first 4 ingredients in a bowl; stir well, and set aside.

2. Beat margarine at medium speed of a mixer until light and fluffy. Gradually add sugar, beating until well blended. Add lemon rind, vanilla, and egg white; beat well. Add flour mixture; stir until well blended. Turn dough out onto wax paper, and shape into a 6-inch log. Wrap log in wax paper, and freeze for 3 hours or until very firm.

3. Preheat oven to 350°.

4. Cut log into 24 (¼-inch-thick) slices, and place slices 1 inch apart on baking sheets coated with cooking spray. Bake at 350° for 8 minutes. Remove cookies from pans, and let cool on wire racks. Yield: 2 dozen (serving size: 1 cookie).

POINTS: 1; **Exchanges:** ½ Starch, ½ Fat
Per serving: CAL 62 (29% from fat); PRO 0.7g; FAT 2g (sat 0.4g); CARB 10.4g; FIB 0.2g; CHOL 0mg; IRON 0.2mg; SOD 50mg; CALC 2mg

Blueberry-Lemon Cheesecake Parfaits

2   (8-ounce) cartons lemon low-fat yogurt
4   ounces tub-style light cream cheese (about ½ cup)
2   tablespoons sifted powdered sugar
1½ cups frozen reduced-calorie whipped topping, thawed
½ cup reduced-fat graham cracker crumbs
1   cup fresh or frozen blueberries, thawed

1. Spoon yogurt onto several layers of heavy-duty paper towels; spread to ½-inch thickness. Cover with additional paper towels; let stand 5 minutes. Scrape yogurt from paper towels into a bowl using a rubber spatula. Add cream cheese and powdered sugar to yogurt, stirring with a whisk until smooth. Fold in whipped topping.

2. Spoon ¼ cup yogurt mixture into each of 6 (4-ounce) parfait glasses. Sprinkle each with 1 tablespoon graham cracker crumbs. Spoon blueberries evenly into each glass. Top each with ¼ cup yogurt mixture and 1 teaspoon crumbs. Serve immediately, or cover and chill until ready to serve. Yield: 6 servings.

POINTS: 4; **Exchanges:** 2 Starch, 1 Fat
Per serving: CAL 205 (30% from fat); PRO 6.5g; FAT 6.9g (sat 2.4g); CARB 30g; FIB 1.2g; CHOL 16mg; IRON 0.3mg; SOD 232mg; CALC 46mg

Fudgy Chocolate Brownies

The technique for these brownies is a bit unorthodox. When you add the sugar and cocoa to the melted chocolate, it forms a ball that's hard to stir. But stick with it; the end result is well worth it.

3   large egg whites
1   large egg

5 tablespoons stick margarine
1 ounce unsweetened chocolate
⅔ cup Dutch process or unsweetened cocoa
1½ cups sugar
1 cup all-purpose flour
½ teaspoon baking powder
Cooking spray

1. Preheat oven to 325°.

2. Combine egg whites and egg in a large bowl; stir well with a whisk, and set aside.

3. Melt margarine and chocolate in a large saucepan over medium heat. Stir in cocoa; cook 1 minute. Stir in sugar, and cook 1 minute (mixture will almost form a ball and be difficult to stir). Remove pan from heat; let cool slightly. Gradually add warm chocolate mixture to eggs, stirring constantly with a whisk until well blended. Combine flour and baking powder; add to chocolate mixture, stirring well.

4. Spoon batter into a 9-inch square baking pan coated with cooking spray. Bake at 325° for 30 minutes (do not overbake). Let cool on a wire rack. Yield: 20 servings.

POINTS: 3; **Exchanges:** 1½ Starch, ½ Fat
Per serving: CAL 132 (29% from fat); PRO 2.5g; FAT 4.3g (sat 1.3g); CARB 21.7g; FIB 0.2g; CHOL 11mg; IRON 0.9mg; SOD 46mg; CALC 16mg

Chewy Chocolate Chip Cookies

2¼ cups all-purpose flour
1 teaspoon baking soda
¼ teaspoon salt
4 large egg whites (at room temperature)
½ cup granulated sugar
⅓ cup light-colored corn syrup
¾ cup firmly packed brown sugar
2 tablespoons light butter (such as Land O' Lakes), softened
1 teaspoon vanilla extract
1¼ cups semisweet chocolate chips
Cooking spray

1. Preheat oven to 375°.

2. Combine first 3 ingredients in a small bowl; stir well, and set aside.

3. Beat egg whites using clean, dry beaters at high speed of a mixer until foamy. Gradually add granulated sugar, 1 tablespoon at a time, beating until soft peaks form. Add corn syrup; beat until stiff peaks form. Set aside.

4. Combine brown sugar, butter, and vanilla extract in a medium bowl; beat at medium speed of a mixer 5 minutes or until well blended. Fold brown sugar mixture into egg white mixture. Fold flour mixture into egg white mixture. Gently stir in chocolate chips.

5. Drop by level tablespoons 1 inch apart onto baking sheets coated with cooking spray. Bake at 375° for 10 minutes or until golden. Remove from oven, and let stand 5 minutes. Remove cookies from pans, and let cool on wire racks. Store loosely covered. Yield: 4 dozen (serving size: 1 cookie).

POINTS: 2; **Exchanges:** 1 Starch
Per serving: CAL 71 (24% from fat); PRO 1.1g; FAT 1.9g (sat 0.9g); CARB 13.1g; FIB 0.2g; CHOL 0.8mg; IRON 0.4mg; SOD 40mg; CALC 5mg

Chewy Chocolate Chip Cookies are great for lunchboxes and after-school snacks.

Each recipe that appears in this cookbook has been through a vigorous testing process and then rated on taste, appearance, and texture. The following recipes received our highest marks. As you use this book, look for the symbol at right, which denotes these top-rated offerings.

Apple Cider-Caramel Cake, 6 *POINTS*, page 88

Bittersweet Chocolate Pudding, 5 *POINTS*, page 82

Chicken Ragout With Pumpkin Dumplings, 8 *POINTS*, page 34

Deviled Chicken Breasts, 5 *POINTS*, page 18

Honey-Grapefruit Granita, 5 *POINTS*, page 89

Hot Maple Soufflés, 4 *POINTS*, page 88

Macaroni and Cheese, 8 *POINTS*, page 23

Make-Ahead Breakfast Casserole, 6 *POINTS*, page 14

Pecan Wild Rice, 7 *POINTS*, page 49

Refrigerator Yeast Rolls, 2 *POINTS*, page 59

White Bean Chili, 7 *POINTS*, page 36

A B O U T   O U R   R E C I P E S

Here are specific guidelines that *Weight Watchers* Magazine adheres to regarding our recipes. For nutritional accuracy, be sure to follow our suggestions.

• When preparing a recipe that yields more than one serving, mix the ingredients well, and then divide the mixture evenly.

• Where liquid and solid parts have to be divided evenly, drain the liquid and set it aside. Evenly divide the remaining ingredients, and then add equal amounts of the liquid to each serving.

• Unless otherwise indicated, servings of meat, poultry, and fish refer to cooked, skinned, and boned servings.

• Recipes provide approximate nutritional information, including the following: CAL (calories), PRO (protein), FAT (total fat), sat (saturated fat), CARB (carbohydrates), FIB (dietary fiber), CHOL (cholesterol), IRON (iron), SOD (sodium), and CALC (calcium). Measurements are abbreviated as follows: g (grams), mg (milligrams).

• Recipes include *POINTS*® based on Weight Watchers International's 1•2•3 Success® Weight Loss Plan.

• *POINTS* are calculated from a formula based on calories, fat, and fiber that assigns higher points to higher-calorie, higher-fat foods. Based on your present weight, you are allowed a certain number of *POINTS* per day.

Note: Because data on fat distribution are not available for some processed foods, these breakdowns should be considered approximate.

• Recipes now include diabetic exchanges, which are calculated from the *Exchange List for Meal Planning* developed by the American Dietetic Association and the American Diabetes Association. The exchange information is designated as follows: starch, fruit, skim milk (sk milk), low-fat milk (l-f milk), whole milk (wh milk), vegetable (veg), very lean meat, lean meat, medium-fat meat (med-fat meat), high-fat meat (hi-fat meat), and fat.

Each category from the exchange list consists of foods that are similar in their nutritional makeup. Therefore, foods within the same category can be substituted. For example, ½ cup cereal for one slice of bread.

• The recipes shown in our photographs may vary as to the number of servings pictured. Please refer to the recipes for the exact serving information.